Candle Making

Candle Making

A Step by Step Guide from Beginner to Expert

Bob Sherman

M. Evans and Co., Inc.
New York

M. Evans and Company, Inc.
216 East 49th Street
New York, New York 10017

Library of Congress Cataloging-in-Publication Data

Sherman, Bob.
    Candle making : from beginner to expert / by Bob Sherman.
        p.   cm.
    ISBN 0-87131-968-3
    1. Candlemaking. I. Title.
TT896.5 .S483 2002
745.593'32—dc21   2001040791

Book design and typesetting by Evan Johnston

Printed in the United States of America

9   8   7   6   5   4   3   2

Contents

Introduction

Candle making—for most of us the very term conjures up vivid images of a colonial family dipping candles in a pot on their hearth or a chandler in a small shop surrounded by hundreds of candles hanging on display. Our imagination is not far from the reality of modern candle making. Although materials and melting techniques have improved, candle making is a skill that has survived relatively unchanged from the dawn of recorded history into the new millennium.

Although candles are a primitive light source, more candles are used today than at any time in history. While candles were originally used by necessity for lighting purposes, today's candles are used primarily for esthetic reasons—mood lighting, fragrance, decoration, symbolism, ritual, and so on.

The world of candle making is fun, exciting, and easy. The creative possibilities for working with wax are endless—the only limit is your imagination. There is a huge variety of candle styles popular today, most originated and perfected through experimentation. Others were discovered by accident. The important thing to remember is that you will learn something new about candle making every time you make one. Aside from safety rules, there are no rules, and you should let your creativity flow.

In the following pages you will discover everything needed to get started in candle making. This book is based on nearly three decades of experience in candle making. Safety, equipment, materials, work area, basic techniques, and a wide variety of step-by-step projects will be covered in an easy-to-understand, non-technical format. I have used this same technique with great success when teaching classes—some of my students have gone from novice to professional after only a class or two.

This book has been laid out sequentially—the projects are ordered from the simplest to the most difficult. Many of the projects build on knowledge acquired by doing previous projects, so I recommend reading and following them in sequence. By doing this you will become a proficient candle maker in the least amount of time. It is important to note here that the difficulty rating on the projects are relative to each other, and even the most difficult is easily mastered with a bit of practice.

1

Understanding Candles

The first step in becoming a proficient candlemaker is to understand how candles work. You may be thinking, "how stupid—everyone knows that you light the wick and the candle burns." Actually the process that allows candles to work in the manner that they do is substantially more complex. Chemistry and physics both play a part, and there is a whole branch of science that studies nothing but flames. Luckily for us, to make good candles, we don't need to know the actual science of it, just the basic concepts. Since this is a how-to book, not a scientific paper, I will leave the technical aspects out and concentrate on the parts that concern us as candlemakers.

The theories discussed here are concepts that I was following unconsciously for many years. It took hours of agonizing thought to actually put them down in a way that could be understood by everyone, not just experienced candle makers. Much of this chapter is a radical departure from conventional "candle wisdom." This is because much of it is original thought, based on experience, not just a repeat of something I read once upon a time.

The Basic Concept

A candle has two primary components: fuel and wick. The fuel is the wax, or, to be more precise, the wax formulation, since usually pure wax is not used. When we light the wick, the heat melts the fuel, and the wick draws the now liquid fuel up to the flame. In turn this produces heat, melting more fuel, thus forming a continuous cycle.

It is as simple as that. From this simple example, we can derive some extremely important concepts as follows:

The wick is not doing most of the actual burning. Its primary function is to supply the flame with fuel. The wick is consumed, but at a very slow rate. You don't have to take my word for it; light a piece of wick without the wax and see how quickly it burns up.

Since a candle is essentially only two components, each is equally important. Think on that for a second. The wick is as important as everything else in the wax put together. *Because it is a continuous cycle, it is vital that the wax melt at the same speed it is consumed by the flame.* If it consumes the wax too fast, it will run out of fuel. If it consumes it too slowly, other problems may occur, such as the wick drowning in its own melt pool.

The Candle as a System

A properly made candle is a good balance between wax, additives, scent, and wick. Changing one ingredient affects all the others, and may require further changes to bring everything back into balance. The individual ingredients used in your candle are not nearly as important as achieving a good balance between the ingredients. *Aside from safety procedures, the single most important factor to remember about your candles is that every material used in a candle affects every other material in the candle.*

Using more or less of a hardener will almost certainly necessitate a wick change. Using more, less, or a different scent may also affect burning and may require a change of wick. Increasing the amount of scent may require the use of Vybar to prevent oil mottling. Changing suppliers of any ingredients will often require adjusting the wick size or wax formula. Recipes are perfected through trial and error. Any change to the base formula should be tested. Usually any adjustments needed for proper burning can be made by changing the wick size.

As you can see from the preceding paragraph, often just changing suppliers of one candle ingredient may necessitate a new round of experimentation and test burning. For best results with a minimum of effort, find suppliers and products you like and stick with them.

2

Candle Making Safety

*C*andle making is a safe pastime; however, it can be very dangerous if you don't follow basic safety precautions. *Please do not attempt to make candles until you have familiarized yourself with this chapter.* Failure to follow the safety rules may result in serious injury to you or your family and damage to your home or workshop. If basic safety precautions are taken, accidental fires should not be a problem, but you must always be prepared since accidents do happen.

SAFETY RULE 1
Never leave melting wax unattended for any reason. Not even in a double boiler or commercially made wax melter. Not for short periods. Not at all. If you must leave the work area for any reason, shut off the heat source.

SAFETY RULE 2
Never overheat wax. The *flash point* is the temperature at which it will spontaneously combust. In plain terms, this means that it will burst

into flames. Spontaneous combustion does not require a spark. Know the flash point of your wax whenever possible. This is usually about 370° F (188° C) for paraffin wax. If you are uncertain of the flash point of your paraffin wax, err on the low side and assume it to be 350° F (177° C). Unless you have a logical reason not to, always heat your wax in a double boiler. This prevents the wax temperature from going above 212° F (100° C), which covers the temperature range required for most candle making. In addition to the danger from fire, the fumes from overheated wax can cause severe illness. In case of an accident evacuate the area and ventilate it.

Safety Rule 3

Always keep wax away from open flame. Wax is a flammable material and as such should not be placed near any heat source. Even if it doesn't catch fire, it may melt.

Safety Rule 4

Always use a thermometer when melting wax. It is essential for safety that you be aware of your wax temperature at all times. A thermometer will also help you achieve good results, and allow you to repeat good results.

Safety Rule 5

Always use a double boiler setup or commercially made wax melter. Temperatures up to 212° F (100° C) can easily be achieved with a double boiler. The vast majority of candle making recipes use a temperature in this range. It is not necessary to use a commercial double boiler. Double boilers will be covered in greater detail in the candle making equipment chapter.

A typical double boiler setup

Very few recipes call for temperatures higher than 200° F (93° C). Those that do will require heating directly on the heat source. This has the potential to be very hazardous. When melting on direct heat you must be very alert. Monitor the wax temperature constantly, and do not allow the temperature to go above 325° F (163° C). Do not let your attention wander for any reason. If possible, do it outdoors on a hot plate.

14

SAFETY RULE 6

Never put water on a wax fire. Wax is an oil product, so it is not water-soluble. Putting water on a wax fire will spatter the flaming wax, creating an even more hazardous situation than you had before. See the last section of this chapter for what to use instead.

SAFETY RULE 7

Always be prepared for a fire. By observing safe candle making practices the chance of a fire is minimized, but you should always be prepared for the worst by having fire-fighting equipment handy. These items should be kept outside of any area that may be affected by fire but still within easy access. I am a firm believer in Murphy's Law (Murphy's Law—anything that can happen, will happen. Usually when you least expect it or are least prepared for it) and feel that the best defense is to be prepared. Fire prevention and preparedness will be covered in greater detail later in this chapter.

NEVER WEAR TIGHT CLOTHES WHEN CANDLE MAKING; LOOSE CLOTHING AND LONG SLEEVES WILL CATCH WAX SPLASHES AND PREVENT BURNS.

SAFETY RULE 8

Always use potholders or pliers when handling hot pots or cans. If wax gets on your skin, run it under cold water immediately, then peel off the wax. It is a smart idea to keep a bucket of water handy so if you splash wax on your hand (the most common place) it can be cooled rapidly by plunging into the water.

SAFETY RULE 9

Never pour wax down the drain. Ignore this only if you want to subsidize your plumber's summer home.

SAFETY RULE 10

Always keep young children and pets out of your work area. At best they are distracting. At worst, they might get hurt. If you are teaching children to make candles, please use common sense and judge on their behavior—not their age. My kids have been proficient candles makers since the age of five, but I know children twice that age who would be dangerous in a candle shop.

SAFETY RULE 11

Never let candle making get so routine that you get careless.

By following these simple safety rules and taking reasonable precautions against fire you will able to relax and enjoy your candle making even more.

Fire Safety

By observing the preceding safety instructions, you should never need to contend with a wax fire. But since we are human, accidents may happen. It is absolutely vital that you be prepared for an accident, just in case. I know many of you are saying, "I'll just be extra careful to prevent accidents," but this is no excuse not to be prepared. Nobody plans on allowing accidents to happen, but they happen anyway.

Never start making candles if you do not have the proper equipment for putting out a fire.

In Case of Fire—DOs

• **Do** put out the fire as quickly as possible. It is vital to put it out before it spreads. If you cannot get it under control, evacuate and call the fire department.

• **Do** shut off the heat source and remove the melting pot to another area to cool.

• **Do** make sure the fire is completely extinguished.

• **Do** ventilate the area—open windows, doors, etc.

• **Do** leave the area until the smoke and fumes dissipate. Overheating wax produces fumes that are unhealthy to breathe.

In Case of Fire—DON'Ts

• **Don't** panic—keep calm.

• **Don't** put water on a wax fire.

• **Don't** breathe the fumes and smoke any longer than necessary to follow the steps above.

Fire Control Equipment

There is very little needed in the way of fire control equipment. The expense is minimal, and the peace of mind is priceless.

Fire Extinguisher

A fire extinguisher is the most important piece of equipment a candle maker can own. Purchase a decent size ABC-type dry chemical fire extinguisher before you make any candles. Your extinguisher should be mounted outside of the wax melting area, yet still close enough to grab fast. Read the instructions on the extinguisher before making your first candles. You will not have time to read them if you have a fire.

Pot Lid

The lid from a cooking pot is also a handy piece of equipment to have. If you have a small wax fire that is confined to the pot, just place the lid on the pot to smother the flame. Although it is not a substitute for a fire extinguisher, this technique is very effective on small melting pot fires.

Baking Soda

Baking soda (sodium bicarbonate) can be used to smother small fires by dumping it on the burning material. Please note that it only works by putting a lot on the fire quickly—it cannot be sprinkled on, so you must have a large supply in a wide-mouth container. I feel this technique is a poor substitute for a fire extinguisher and do not recommend it. I only include it here because I realize that some readers may be in countries where fire extinguishers are difficult to obtain, and baking soda is better than nothing.

3

Candle Measures

$\mathcal{M}$easuring wax and additives is one of the most important parts of candle making. Many beginners become obsessed with high precision in their wax formulas. While precision is a good thing, repeatable results are much more important for success. If you derive great satisfaction from knowing that your formulas are precise to the milligram, by all means do so. But acceptable, repeatable results can also be obtained with a measuring cup and a teaspoon—because you can use the same cup and spoon next time.

This chapter covers the wide range of measurements and conversions you may encounter as a candle maker. At the very least you should read and familiarize yourself with the contents of this chapter. There is no need to memorize it all; you can always refer back to the tables as the need arises. If you are mathemati-

TEASPOONS AND TABLESPOONS REFER TO MEASURING SPOONS, NOT A SPOON YOU WOULD EAT WITH.

cally impaired, don't be alarmed—you don't need to be a math whiz to make good candles. All the recipes in this book are designed to be easy to use, and require only basic math skills.

Common Formula Abbreviations

Most units of measure in formulas are abbreviated. By knowing these abbreviations you can avoid the common mistake of using the wrong measurement. The tables below show the most common abbreviations.

WEIGHT MEASURES	
Ounce	*oz*
Pound	*lb*
Gram (metric)	*g or gm*
Kilogram (metric)	*kg or kilo*

VOLUME MEASURES	
Teaspoon	*tsp*
Tablespoon	*Tbs*
Cup	*c*
Fluid Ounce	*fl oz*
Milliliter (metric)	*ml*
Liter (metric)	*l*

NOTATION	
Equals	=
Approximately	≅
Multiply	× *or* *
Divide	/ *or* ÷
Add	+
Subtract	−
Less than	<
Greater than	>
Percent	%
Degrees	°

A COMMON MISTAKE AMONG
BEGINNERS IS CONFUSING
TEASPOONS WITH
TABLESPOONS.

Scales

The most accurate way to work with candle making supplies is by weight. Weights are usually given in pounds and ounces, but may be in grams and kilograms (metric). If you have a scale, recipes are much easier to work with. A scale allows much more accurate measurements, providing more exact repeatability. It is important to note that if you usually work with small batches of wax, you will need a more accurate scale since you will need to measure smaller quantities of most ingredients.

If you plan to buy a scale, I recommend purchasing a laboratory-type scale. Diet and postage scales tend to be substantially less accurate. My personal preference for average candle making is a digital scale with a capacity of 2 kilograms (4.4 pounds). Most scales in this range will weigh to about 1 gram (0.035 ounce). This covers all but the tiniest measurements you will need. Digital scales have many advantages over mechanical scales (balance or triple beam). They give a reading faster— no waiting for the scale to balance. Most digital scales can be set to ounces or grams, while mechanical scales are usually only in grams (metric). With a digital scale, the weight of a container can be deducted (tared) at the push of a button. To tare a mechanical scale takes a lot more effort. The main disadvantage of digital scales is that they are relatively fragile compared to mechanical scales.

If you find a need for *exact* repeatability, much more accurate scales are available. These generally have a much smaller capacity (100 to 400 grams is typical), but they will measure as little as 0.01 or even 0.001 grams. I keep one of these in my shop for measuring dye when I need to make multiple batches with identical color.

Larger capacity scales are available, but they generally have a substantially lower accuracy and thus they are not well suited to weighing small amounts. Since any amount may be weighed out in smaller batches, I consider these a luxury unless you weigh larger quantities often enough to justify the time savings (for example, if you need 6 pounds but only have a 4-pound capacity scale, you could just weigh out 3 pounds twice to get 6 pounds).

If your budget doesn't have room for a scale, there are alternative measuring methods. These will be explained in the next section.

Converting Weight to Volume Measures

If you don't have a scale, the following can often be used to get an approximate equivalent good enough for a working recipe. For example, by looking at the chart below you will see that 2 tablespoons equals approximately 1 ounce (28.3 ml) of liquid. Be aware that volume measures are based on the weight of water, so unless you are weighing water this is not a very accurate way to measure. Most candle products are oil based, and oil is lighter than water. The true weight when measured this way will be slightly less than calculated. These measures may also be used with melted wax, although they are very inaccurate with solid wax.

DO NOT CONFUSE FLUID OUNCES WITH WEIGHED OUNCES.

APPROXIMATE WEIGHT TO VOLUME CONVERSIONS

1 pound ≅	16 fl oz	454 ml	96 tsp	32 Tbs
1 ounce ≅	1 fl oz	28.3 ml	6 tsp	2 Tbs
1 gram ≅			⅕ tsp	

Volume Measures with Solids

Volume measures work differently with solid material than they do with liquids. This is because there is more air and less material (the technical term is less density). A good example of this is Vybar, which weighs approximately ⅑ ounce per level teaspoon. A teaspoon of a liquid weighs approximately ⅙ ounce. The table below shows the typical weight of various candle making products. If you are using a product not shown, find a similar product and use the weight shown.

APPROXIMATE WEIGHT OF VOLUME MEASURES OF SOLIDS

Vybar	1 teaspoon ≅	⅑ oz	3.2 g
Stearic acid	1 teaspoon ≅	⅓ oz	8.7 g
Luster crystals	1 teaspoon ≅	⅑ oz	3.2 g

Weighing Wax Without a Scale

Wax is usually purchased in either slabs or granulated form. A fairly accurate weight can be obtained with the following techniques.

Measuring Slab Wax

Slab wax is typically sold in 10.3 pound slabs. To weigh it without a scale, a yardstick and a sharp object can be used. Mark the centerline lengthwise by measuring the center then scribing a line. Next use the yardstick to divide the slab into 5 equal pieces (perpendicular to the center line) and scribe lines. By breaking the slab up as close to the lines as possible, you will have ten pieces, each about one pound. If you have a 12-pound slab, just divide into twelve equal pieces.

Measuring Granulated Wax

Granulated wax comes in a variety of textures ranging from sugar size granules to large pastilles. Because of this there will be some variation in weight when measuring with this technique—smaller granules will usually provide a more accurate measurement. Use an 8-fluid-ounce (227 ml or 1 cup) measuring cup. Because of the density of the wax, one level cupful will equal approximately 4 ounces (114 grams) of wax by weight. This is another weight to volume conversion, so there is no direct correlation between the ounce capacity of the cup and the weight in ounces.

BE CAREFUL WITH DECIMAL POINT PLACEMENT.

Metric Conversion

The metric system has been adopted by most of the world, but here in the United States most of us are still using inches, ounces, and Farenheit. The metric system is easier to use, if you are used to it, since it is based on multiples of ten (much like United States currency). Since I have used English measurements all my life, I am most comfortable working in that system and cannot easily convert metric into English measurements without a calculator. The following table contains the necessary formulas for converting between the two systems, should you need to.

English to Metric Conversion

To change	to	multiply by
Inches	millimeters	25.4
Inches	centimeters	25.4
Ounces	grams	28.34
Pounds	kilograms	0.4536
Fluid ounces	milliliters	29.574

Metric to English Conversion

To change	to	multiply by
Millimeters	inches	0.0394
Centimeters	inches	0.3937
Grams	ounces	0.0353
Kilograms	pounds	2.2046
Milliliters	fluid ounces	0.03

Metric Equivalents for Common Volume Measures

Teaspoon	5 milliliters
Tablespoon	15 milliliters
Fluid ounce	30 milliliters
Cup	0.24 liter
Pint	0.47 liter
Quart	0.95 liter

Temperature Conversions

In the Farenheit system water freezes at 32° and boils at 212°. In Celsius water freezes at 0° and boils at 100°. Converting from Farenheit to Celsius or vice versa is slightly more complex than other metric conversions. There is no number that can simply be multiplied to obtain a conversion since the difference between the two systems is greater at higher temperatures (only a 32-degree difference at freezing, but a 112-degree difference at boiling). If you are good with math you may wish to do these conversions on paper, but a calculator makes it much easier.

Farenheit to Celsius

Farenheit Temperature $- 32 \times \frac{5}{9} =$ *Celsius Temperature*

or (if you are using a calculator)

Farenheit Temperature $- 32 \times 0.556 =$ *Celsius Temperature*

Example:
185° F $- 32 \times \frac{5}{9} = 85°$ C

Celsius to Farenheit

Celsius Temperature $\times \frac{9}{5} + 32 =$ *Farenheit Temperature*

or (if you are using a calculator)

Celsius Temperature $\times 1.8 + 32 =$ *Farenheit Temperature*

Example:
73° C $\times \frac{9}{5} + 32 = 163.4°$ F

Measure Equivalents

In the metric system it is very obvious how quantities relate to each other. For example, we can tell at a glance that 100 grams is half of 200 grams, and double 50 grams. It is a little more confusing with cups, teaspoons, and other English measurements. The table below shows the relationship between all of the common sizes of volume measuring tools.

ENGLISH TO METRIC CONVERSION			
1 teaspoon	0.17 fl oz		
1 teaspoon	0.5 fl oz	3 tsp	
1 cup	8 fl oz	48 tsp	16 Tbs
1 pint	16 fl oz	96 tsp	32 Tbs
1 quart	32 fl oz	192 tsp	64 Tbs
1 gallon	128 fl oz	768 tsp	256 Tbs

Formula Types

Most wax formulas you encounter will be one of three types: recipe, percentage, or proportional.

Recipe Formulas

This is the most common type of wax formula. I call these formulas "recipe formulas" because they are very much like cooking recipes. Of all the formula types, they are the easiest to work with, so the formulas in this book are all recipe type. These formulas are typically given as one pound of wax plus additives. To mix larger batches, just multiply each ingredient.
    Example:

1 pound 140° F (60° C) wax
1 teaspoon Vybar 103
1 ounce scent oil
Dye to desired color

To make 4 pounds of this formula, simply multiply each ingredient by 4 to get:

4 pounds 140° F (60° C) wax
4 teaspoons Vybar 103
4 ounce scent oil
Dye to desired color

Percentage Formulas

This type of formula is much less common, and although these formulas are simple, they are not quite as easy to follow as recipe formulas. A major advantage of percentage formulas is that they work equally well with any measuring system. One percent is one hundreth of anything whether you are measuring in kilos, pounds, fluid ounces, milliliters, etc. One percent can be represented mathematically as $\frac{1}{100}$ or 0.01. Eleven percent would be $\frac{11}{100}$ or 0.11, and so on. If you have a calculator that does percentages it is even easier. Take care with decimal point placement as there is a big difference between 1, 0.1, and 0.01 True percentage formulas always add up to 100 percent. But this is more complex than is necessary for most candle making.

Example of a true percentage formula:

93½% (0.935) paraffin wax
½% (0.005) Vybar
6% (0.06) fragrance oil

Total = 100%

If we wanted to make ten pounds of this formula, we would multiply 10 times 0.935 for the paraffin, 10 times 0.005 for the Vybar, and 10 times 0.06 for the scent oil. Giving us 9.35 pounds of paraffin, 0.05 pounds of Vybar, and 0.6 pounds of scent oil. As you can see, this is fairly straightforward math, but if you don't have a scale, measuring 9.35 pounds will be difficult.

Most percentage formulas are given as a percentage of the wax to simplify things. By doing this we can pick a nice even number of pounds of paraffin wax.

Example of percentage of wax formula:

> 10 pounds paraffin wax
> ½% (0.005) Vybar
> 6% (0.06) fragrance oil

If we wanted to make ten pounds of this formula, we would multiply 10 times 0.005 for the Vybar, and 10 times 0.06 for the scent oil, giving us 10 pounds of paraffin, 0.05 pounds of Vybar, and 0.6 pounds of scent oil.

These results can be converted into any unit of measure before or after calculating. It is generally easier to convert before calculating.

Example: To calculate the previous example in grams, multiply 10×454 (1 pound = 454 grams as determined by the metric conversion table). This gives us 4,540 grams of paraffin, $4,540 \times 0.005 = 22.7$ grams of Vybar, and $4,540 \times 0.06 = 272.4$ grams of scent.

COMMON PERCENTAGE EQUIVALENTS PER POUND

Percentage	Weight (oz)	Weight (g)	Volume (tsp)	Volume (Tbs)
½%	0.08	2.27	≅ ½	
1%	0.16	4.54	≅ 1	
2%	0.32	9.08	≅ 2	
3%	0.48	13.62	≅ 3	≅ 1
4%	0.64	18.16	≅ 4	
5%	0.80	22.7	≅ 5	
6%	0.96	27.24	≅ 6	≅ 2
7%	1.12	31.78	≅ 7	
8%	1.28	36.32	≅ 8	
9%	1.44	40.86	≅ 9	≅ 3
10%	1.6	45.4	≅ 10	
15%	2.4	68.1	≅ 15	≅ 5
20%	3.2	90.8	≅ 20	
25%	4.0	113.5	≅ 25	

The most important use for percentages is for adding an additive not included in the recipe (such as release wax, ultraviolet inhibitor, etc.). Most suppliers recommend they be added at a certain percentage, although some will include volume measures as well.

Proportional Formulas

This is the least common, and least well understood type of formula. Oddly enough, it is a very simple type to use. Any unit of measure may be used, as long as the same unit is used for each ingredient.

Example of a proportional formula:

> *90 parts paraffin*
> *10 parts stearic acid*
> *1 part release wax*
> *8 parts fragrance oil*

If we use ounces, each ingredient is multiplied by 1 ounce. This gives us 90 ounces of paraffin, 10 ounces of stearic acid, 1 ounce release wax, 8 ounces of fragrance oil, for a total of 109 ounces of wax formula.

If we only wanted 50 ounces of this formula it can be scaled down. Dividing the 109 by 50 to get 2.18. Each ingredient is then divided by 2.18 to give us 41.28 ounces of paraffin, 4.59 ounces of stearic acid, .46 ounces of release wax, and 3.67 ounces of fragrance oil.

The formula can also be scaled up. To convert this to a 170 ounces formula, divide 170 by 109 to get 1.56. Each ingredient is then multiplied by 1.56

Converting Proportional Formulas to Percentage Formulas

If you normally work with percentage formulas, you may wish to convert a proportional formula. The mathematical formula for this is (parts ÷ total parts) × 100 = percentage.

From the example above we have 90 parts of paraffin and 109 total parts. Plug these numbers into the conversion formula and we get (90 ÷ 109) × = 82.57 percent. This is repeated for each ingredient.

4

Candle Making Equipment

The amount of equipment you need to get started is minimal. Many of the items needed are normal food preparation items. Much of it can be found at garage sales, thrift shops, or dollar stores. Some you may already have at home. You should be aware that most equipment used for candle making will no longer be useable for food preparation. If you take good care of your equipment it will last a long time, so money spent on equipment can be considered a one-time expense.

Fire Extinguisher

It is no accident that the first item listed here is a dry chemical fire extinguisher. It is the most important piece of candle making equipment that you can own. Oddly enough, it is also the piece of equipment that you are least likely to ever use. Please refer to chapter 2 for more information.

Melting Equipment

The next item needed will be something to melt the wax in. The safest way to melt wax is in a double boiler. This may be a commercial double boiler, but most people make their own. The simplest way is to place a small pot containing wax inside a larger pot that has a couple of inches of water in the bottom of it.

Many candle supply companies sell what is called a pouring pot This is an aluminum pot with a pour spout and heat resistant handle, which is very convenient for both melting and pouring wax. The wax is placed in the pour-

Pouring Pot

ing pot, which is then set inside a larger pot containing water. Although pouring pots are very convenient, if you are on a tight budget any pot will do. A coffee can will also work, but since they are not seamless they will eventually leak (usually at the most inopportune moment).

Another option is a commercial wax melter. Although very convenient, these are generally much larger than the average hobbyist needs. They take a long time to heat up and carry a big price tag. If you are not in the candle business, they are generally not worth the expense.

Heat Source

Unless you are using a commercial wax melter, it will be necessary to have some way to heat your double boiler. For most this is as simple as the kitchen stovetop. If that is not an option, then an electric hot plate will suffice. Although recently I have heard of companies advocating the use of a microwave oven for melting wax, I do not consider this a safe option.

Thermometer

A good thermometer is necessary for both safety and quality purposes. The type of thermometer designed to clip on the side

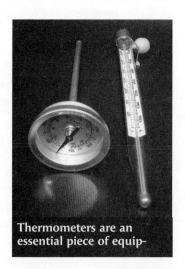

Thermometers are an essential piece of equip-

of a pot is best. There are thermometers made just for candle making, but any candy or deep-fry thermometer will work. When selecting a thermometer, make sure it will read temperatures between 100 and 400° F.

Most thermometers of this type will be either glass or metal. Although the glass type are more fragile, they are usually longer, enabling you to get an easy temperature reading with as little as one pound of wax in the pot. Metal thermometers are much more durable, but tend to have shorter shafts.

Molds

Most candle making is done in molds (unless you only plan to make dipped or container candles). There are a large variety of molds available in a wide range of materials. common mold materials are plastic, acrylic, rubber, aluminum, and sheet metal.

Candle molds are available in a wide variety of sizes, shapes, and materials.

Plastic Molds

The least expensive molds are usually made of plastic. These may be as simple as a one-piece open-topped mold, or as complex as a two-piece mold. These are generally pretty durable and will last for hundreds of candles with minimal care, but durability varies with the actual plastic used to make the mold.

Scent oils, release compounds, and mold cleaners may affect some plastic molds. To avoid ruining the mold, these should be tested on the outside of the mold before use on the inside.

One-Piece

One-piece plastic molds are sometimes called open top molds or tray molds. These are most commonly used for making wax appliqués, but there are some available that are deep enough for candles.

Two-Piece

Two-piece plastic molds are usually used to create designs with undercuts or odd shapes. Many novelty candles are made with two-piece plastic molds. Two-piece molds need to be clamped together and placed in a stand. Most two-piece molds do not come with clamps or a stand to hold them upright when pouring, and these will need to be purchased separately. Recently there have been some designs introduced that have the clamping system built in and are wide enough to stand on their own, but there is a fairly small selection of these on the market.

Acrylic Molds

Acrylic is a common material for pillar candle molds. These are easily identified because they are clear. The major advantage of these is being able to see what is happening inside the mold. Acrylic does not take scented wax well and today's heavily scented candles will often ruin acrylic molds after a few pourings. If you plan to make scented candles I suggest avoiding acrylic molds.

Rubber Molds

There are a variety of rubbers used to make candle molds. The most common are silicone, latex, and polyurethane. They all have advantages and disadvantages, which will be explained below.

Silicone

Silicone is a great mold material. It is self-lubricating, durable, and impervious to almost everything. Unfortunately, it is also relatively expensive. Although it has a low flexibility, it is ideal for making two-piece or split molds. Silicone molds will leave a nearly invisible seam that shouldn't require trimming.

Latex

Latex rubber is relatively inexpensive and very flexible. It is commonly used to make seamless molds, which are peeled or rolled off the finished candle. Due to their flexibility they usually need to be supported, as they will not stay upright on their own. The main disadvantages to latex molds are that they not very durable and they are susceptible to damage from some candle making products such as stearic. Another disadvantage of many latex molds is their affinity for candle dye. They will often absorb dye from the candles made in them, and then release the dye onto subsequently poured candles. While sometimes this appearance is desirable, usually it is not. To extend the life of your latex molds, they should be washed thoroughly with soapy water before storing.

Polyurethane

Polyurethane falls somewhere between latex and silicone in price and durability. It is not quite as durable as silicone, but much longer lasting than latex. Molds made with polyurethane are similar to silicone in appearance. As with latex, a disadvantage of polyurethanes is their affinity for candle dye. They will absorb dye from the candles made in them, and often release the dye onto subsequently poured candles.

Aluminum Molds

Candle manufacturers have been using one-piece seamless aluminum molds for years, but recently they have become more widely available to the general public. This is my favorite type of mold, although the selection available is not as good as for other molds. Aluminum molds are very durable, do not rust, and—best of all—no seam trimming is ever needed. They also produce a nice surface finish without using a water bath. Although aluminum is a metal, I have listed these separately since they are seamless.

Metal Molds

This category of molds is the largest, and there is a huge selection with many interesting sizes and shapes to choose from. Most molds of this type are sheet metal that has been formed to shape, then soldered to keep the seams from leaking. The main drawback to these molds is the seam. The seam is not a problem on any mold shape with an edge, such as squares, stars, and pyramids, since the seam is on a corner. On round and oval molds there is no corner, and the seam will need to be trimmed from the finished candle. Molds of this type usually will provid a better surface finish when used with a water bath. Water baths will be covered in detail in chapter 10.

Some molds in this category are seamless, such as votive and floating candle molds. These are typically stamped out of thin-gauge metal in one piece. It is not uncommon for metal molds to have sharp edges, and care should be used when handling them.

Chocolate Molds

Chocolate or candy molds are sometimes used for candle making and appliqué work. Unlike plastic molds designed for candle making, the plastic used in these molds is much more heat sensitive. Most will distort or sag from temperatures as low as 165° F (74° C). It is very important to be aware of your wax temperature when working with chocolate molds.

Found Molds

Many of us remember making candles in milk cartons as part of a school or scout project, but the only limit to what you can use for candle molds is your imagination. If you look around your home, many potential molds will be found—film cans, juice concentrate containers, cups, glasses, jars, etc.

When looking to make molds from found objects they need to meet a few criteria:

- Will it hold wax?
- Will it withstand the necessary pouring temperature?
- Will the candle come out once hardened? Or can the mold be removed from the candle (such as peeling off a milk carton).

Measuring Tools

An inexpensive set of measuring spoons will be needed. It is best to purchase a set of metal measuring spoons, as these are easier to wipe clean and will not absorb scent. Typical sizes needed will range from ⅛ teaspoon to 1 tablespoon (approximately .79 to 4.71 ml).

A basic set of measuring spoons will suffice for the beginner.

A scale is handy to have, as it can make much more accurate measurements, but it is not a necessity for the beginner. There are ways to "weigh" items without a scale, which we've covered in chapter 3.

Miscellaneous

Potholders

Since we are going to be working with hot pots, it is usually helpful to keep a few potholders or oven mitts handy.

Scissors

Aside from the obvious uses for a pair of scissors, they are handy for cutting and trimming wicks. Please note that they should not be used to trim wire-cored wick as this will dull and eventually ruin the scissors.

Wire Cutters

A good quality pair of wire cutters is handy for cutting and trimming wire-cored wicks. These may also be used in place of scissors to cut non-cored wick.

A narrow point wire cutter works best.

Knife

I keep a variety of knives on my workbench, ranging from a small hobby knife with a #11 blade up to a heavy utility knife. There are all sorts of uses for knives from trimming seams, and shaving dye blocks to opening wax cartons.

Wooden Spoons

Wooden spoons are useful for stirring the wax in the melting pot and for tapping mold sides to release air bubbles when necessary. Try to obtain long spoons, as many of the lower quality wooden spoons are too short. I keep two spoons in my melting area. One is used only for white and ivory wax, and the other is used for colored wax.

Pliers

The main use for pliers is crimping wick tabs. They are also handy if melting in a container without a handle such as a coffee can. The pliers can be used when handling the hot can.

Mold Weights

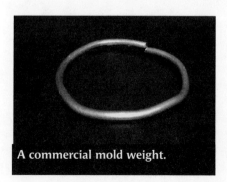
A commercial mold weight.

When using a water bath, mold weights are used to keep the mold from floating or tipping over. Since wax is lighter than water, the mold will be slightly buoyant in the water, and a little weight is needed to prevent this. Commercial mold weights are lead and are soft enough to wrap around the base of the mold. They are easily moved from mold to mold. If you don't to have a commercial mold weight, a length of chain wrapped around the mold and held together with wire or a paper clip will work. Lead is toxic, and you should immediately wash your hands thoroughly with soap and water after handling lead mold weights.

Hammer and Chisel

Since most wax is supplied in slab form, a hammer and chisel is used to break it up. Any type of hammer will do. The best chisel is a 1-inch (2.5 cm) wide carpenter's chisel, but any chisel will do. In a pinch you could even use a large screwdriver.

Pans

A variety of inexpensive baking pans and cookie sheets come in handy for many projects (such as chunk candles). These also make handy receptacles for leftover wax.

5

Candle Making Materials

*I*n this chapter all the materials required to make candles will be discussed. No other aspect of candle making has changed as much in recent years as the materials used to make them. Although many of the materials used today have been around for a long time, there have been improvements in quality on many, as well as a variety of new products that make it easier than ever to produce high quality candles.

One of the most common questions asked by beginning candle makers is, "How do I know which materials to choose from the huge variety available?" The answer always depends on the type of candle you wish to make. Familiarizing yourself with what products are available and their general uses, you will take much of the mystery out of selecting materials. The projects and recipes presented in this book each include a materials list, but when experimenting or using projects from another source it is helpful to have a basic understanding of when and why you are using them.

Waxes

The sheer number of different waxes currently available can be daunting to those just getting started. High melt point, low melt point, one-pour, microcrystalline, beeswax, wax art crystals, and many other names will be encountered. Since most of us have never encountered any of these terms in everyday life, it all sounds quite mystifying to the beginner. The following is an explanation of the various common waxes and their typical uses.

Paraffin Wax

The most common wax used in candle making is paraffin. Paraffin is a petroleum oil product and is closely related to gasoline, kerosene, and petroleum jelly. Petroleum refining is well beyond the scope of this book, and all we need to know is that paraffin wax can be manipulated during manufacture to provide us with a wide range of properties. Paraffin wax was introduced to the candle making industry in the mid-1800s and has grown in popularity to the

Paraffin is usually supplied in slab form, but is available in granulated form from some suppliers.

point where today the vast majority of candles are made with it.

Paraffin wax is most commonly distinguished by its melting point (also referred to as MP), which is also the most important property for candle makers. Melting point is a useful reference when determining the suitability of a given wax for a specific type of candle. The second most important property of paraffin wax is its oil content. Although there are many properties in the specifications sheet for waxes, I advise you not to get too wrapped up in the technical aspects. If the wax works well for your purpose, use it. If not, try a different wax.

WAX FROM DIFFERENT SOURCES MAY HAVE THE SAME MELT POINT, BUT DIFFER IN OTHER PROPERTIES.

It is important to note that the specifications for most properties of paraffin wax have a fairly broad tolerance. For example: a 121° F (49° C) melting point wax may actually have a melting point in the range of 120 to 125° F (48 to 52° C). This will not have any effect to us as candle makers.

Paraffin wax is most commonly supplied in slabs ranging from 10 to 13 pounds, but it is available from some suppliers in pastille or granulated form.

Low Melting Point Paraffin Waxes

Generally, paraffin waxes with a melting point of 130° F (54° C) or less are considered to be low melting point waxes. Many of these tend to have a higher oil content than other waxes. These are usually used for container candles and votive candles. Waxes at the lowest portion of this range—around 120° F (48° C) are generally only suitable for container candles, and even then are often blended with a higher melting point wax to get a melt point somewhere in between.

Medium Melting Point Paraffin Waxes

Paraffin waxes with a melting point of 131 to 145° F (55 to 63° C) are usually referred to as medium melting point waxes. Most so-called "general purpose" waxes are in this range. Most molded candle making is done with wax in this range, with 140 to 145° F (60 to 63° C) melting point being my preferred choice.

High Melting Point Paraffin Waxes

Paraffin waxes with a melting point above 145° F (63° C) are considered high melting point waxes. These generally have a lower oil content than other waxes and are best suited for use where high heat resistance is needed.

Beeswax

The second most popular candle making wax is beeswax. Beeswax is a natural product extracted from honeybee hives. Most beeswax has a melting point of about 145° F (63° C). It has a pleasant honey smell, and is available in a variety of forms. The natural color ranges from pale yellow through amber, and it is also available in bleached white. Although usually sold in block form, it can also be purchased in thin sheets that have been dyed a wide variety of colors.

RAW BEESWAX MAY BE CLEANED BY MELTING, THEN POURING THROUGH CHEESE-CLOTH.

The quality of beeswax varies greatly depending on how it was processed. Smaller producers of beeswax usually do not have the equipment necessary to fully separate the honey from the wax; however, if you are willing to put a bit more time into preparing the wax for use, this is usually the least

Bulk beeswax is usually supplied in blocks and is available in natural or bleached color.

expensive way to purchase beeswax. Larger producers have the equipment necessary to fully separate the honey, but usually charge higher prices for the wax.

It is commonly believed that adding beeswax to paraffin will improve candle quality. This may have been true at one time, but my experience has shown that a well made paraffin candle will burn just as well as one containing a paraffin/beeswax blend (and at a much lower cost). Due to its properties, beeswax is well suited to many applications—rolled sheet candles, all-natural candles, hanging wax ornaments, and appliqués to name but a few.

Following a long-standing tradition, most churches require their candles to be at least 51 percent beeswax, and some churches actually will only use 100-percent beeswax candles. This dates back to a time when most candles were made with tallow, which smells quite bad and smokes when burning.

Blended Waxes

There are a variety of pre-blended waxes on the market. These are ready-to-use wax formulations designed to be used for specific candle types. There are blended waxes available for most types of candles. Although usually more expensive than pure paraffin wax, they usually contain everything needed except color and fragrance. As with anything else, some are very good and some are not. I recommend you try a small amount to see how you like it before committing to a volume purchase if this type of wax interests you.

One-Pour Waxes

These are also known as single-pour waxes. These are blended waxes that are designed for minimum shrinkage when poured into container candles. I personally have not liked the burning properties of any of the one-pour waxes I have tried as of this writing, but many folks are quite happy with them, so if they interest you, by all means try them. The term "one-pour" is something of a misnomer, because it is not unusual to need a second pour with them—especially in large containers. They do, however, shrink far less than more traditional wax formulas.

Wax Crystals

These are also a form of blended wax. Wax crystals are usually made with paraffin, hardener, and dye that has been granulated. Although these may be melted and poured, they are usually used in granulated form (for projects similar to sand art). Do not confuse these with granulated pure paraffin.

Bayberry Wax

Bayberry wax is a natural wax extracted from bayberries. Burning bayberry candles is supposed to bring good luck. The most popular form of bayberry candle is a dipped taper, and there is even a poem that goes with them (see sidebar). Commercially prepared bayberry wax is quite expensive, although if you have access to a bayberry bush it is simple to make your own. The berries are boiled in water; the wax will separate and float to the surface where it can be skimmed off.

"THE BAYBERRY CANDLE IS A GIFT FROM A FRIEND. ON CHRISTMAS EVE BURN IT DOWN TO THE END. FOR A BAYBERRY CANDLE BURNED TO THE SOCKET, BRINGS JOY TO YOUR LIFE AND WEALTH TO YOUR POCKET."

Microcrystalline Wax

Microcrystalline waxes are paraffin waxes whose molecular structure has been altered. There are quite a few different types with a broad range of properties. These waxes are generally used as additives and will be covered in more detail later in this chapter.

Vegetable Wax

This category covers a variety of waxy formulations based on vegetable oils instead of petroleum oil. These are a recent development in the candle industry, and as of this writing there is not much data available about them. They are still difficult to find and have not achieved widespread acceptance. I mention them here because I feel they may someday be a major factor in the candle industry. Those who wish to produce totally non-animal or all-natural candles may wish to experiment with them, although I suggest beginners stick to more traditional materials.

Synthetic Wax

Recent years have seen the introduction of some synthetic waxes. These are also a recent development in the candle industry, and as of this writing there is very little data available about them. Like vegetable waxes, they are still difficult for the average candle maker to find and are mentioned here because I feel they may someday be a major factor in the candle industry. Those who wish to experiment with them should, since most of the huge body of candle making information now available derives from people experimenting. Again, I suggest beginners stick to more traditional materials.

Additives

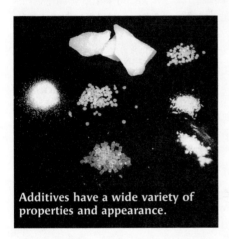

Additives have a wide variety of properties and appearance.

The candle maker of today has a much better choice of additives than even those of ten years ago did. Candle technology has advanced by leaps and bounds in recent years. With the current popularity of candles, we can probably expect many more advances in the next few years.

I am a strong advocate of experimentation but try not to get caught up in what I call "Complex Formula Syndrome" or CFS. Candle makers suffering from this common problem seem to be under the misconception that a wax formula has to have many ingredients to be any good. In reality the opposite is true—simple formulas work best. The easiest way to avoid CFS is to make sure you have a good, logical reason for adding something to your wax before using it.

Stearic Acid

Stearic acid can be considered the first additive developed for candles. It was first discovered in the early 1800s. By the mid-1800s it was being combined with paraffin wax to make candles similar to those made today. The term is used interchangeably with *stearin* and *stearine*. Most often it is just referred to as *stearic*. It is still the most readily available candle additive, and can be found wherever candle making supplies are sold.

Stearic acid is used primarily to harden the wax. Additionally, it makes the wax opaque and provides a nicer surface finish. It usually works best at a rate of 3 tablespoons per pound of wax (95 ml per kilo), although it can be used in much larger quantities with no ill effect to the candle. It can be placed into the melting pot with the wax, as it melts in the same temperature range.

Stearic is available in two forms—animal based and vegetable based. The animal based is derived from the byproducts of food production (animal fat). Vegetable based stearic is usually derived from palm leaves. Both work equally well, and I have never been able to tell the difference in finished candles. Additionally, there are various grades commonly available—single pressed, double pressed, or triple pressed. I can see no major difference in the finished candle with any of these, but since the difference in price is minimal I usually use double or triple pressed.

Vybar

Vybar is a relatively recent addition to the candle maker's arsenal of additives. A polymer that is produced by Baker Petrolite Corporation, Vybar does amazing things for candles. Although not quite as easy to find as stearic acid, it is well worth the effort to obtain. You will probably not find it at your local craft store, but it can be mail ordered from most full-line candle supply companies.

Vybar is used to harden the wax, increase opacity, improve fragrance (on scented candles), and inhibit mottling. It is available in two types. Vybar 103 has a melting point of 160° F (71° C) and is generally used with waxes having a melting point of 140° F or higher. Vybar 103 is a white color. Vybar 260 has a melting point of 130° F (54° C) and is usually used for applications requiring a low melt point such as container candles. Vybar 260 is an off-white color.

Typical usage is one teaspoon per pound (10 ml. per kilo) of wax, although it can be used in smaller quantities. Usage at quantities as high as 2 teaspoons per pound will cause surface ripples. Vybar can be placed into the melting pot with the wax, as it melts in the same temperature range.

Luster Crystals

Luster crystals are another relatively new additive. They are in the polythene family and are used to harden wax, increase opacity, and improve surface finish. I have seen different companies market different products as luster crystals, so don't assume that you are getting the same product when ordering from different suppliers.

Typical usage is one quarter-teaspoon to one teaspoon per pound (2.5 to 10 ml per kilo) of wax. Luster crystals usually have a melting point above 200° F (93° C), so they need to be melted separately. This is done with a second melting pot containing a small quantity of wax is heated on direct heat—using extreme caution (please refer to the chapter on safety to refresh your memory before using direct heat). Once fully melted, the mixture is stirred thoroughly into the melted wax in your double boiler.

Clear Crystals

Clear crystals are also a relatively new additive. Like luster crystals, they are also in the polythene family, but these crystals are used to harden wax and improve surface finish without increasing opacity. Different companies market different products as clear crystals, so don't assume that you are getting the same product when ordering from a different supplier.

Typical usage is one quarter-teaspoon to one teaspoon per pound (2.5 to 10 ml. per kilo) of wax. Clear crystals usually have a melting point well above 200° F (93° C), so they need to be melted separately. This is done with a second melting pot containing a small quantity of wax as explained for luster crystals.

Micro 180

This is a microcrystalline additive used to harden wax without increasing opacity. There are a variety of high melting point microcrystalline waxes that can be used for the same purpose, although they may be marketed under other names. Micro 180 is added when a very hard yet translucent wax is desired, such as for a hurricane candles. These are normally melted with the wax. Typical usage ranges from one percent to twenty percent, depending on the degree of hardness desired.

Tacky Wax

Tacky wax is also a microcrystalline wax. Although sold under a variety of names, it is also commonly marketed as "taper hold wax." It has a variety of uses, but as an additive it is sometimes added to dipping wax to improve layer adhesion. The most common usage is not as an additive, but as an adhesive. Since it remains tacky, it has good adhesion and is commonly used as a glue to apply things to candles.

When used as an additive, typical usage ranges from one percent to ten percent. When used as an adhesive it can be smeared on straight from the block, or melted and brushed on. The same property that makes it so useful also makes it very annoying to use—it sticks to everything.

Other Microcrystalline Waxes

The sheer variety of microcrystalline waxes makes it impossible to list them all. It is just important to be aware that there are quite a few available with a broad range of properties. Microcrystalline waxes are relatively difficult to find, although most full-line candle supply companies stock at least a few.

Ultraviolet Inhibitors

AT A CRAFT SHOW, I ONCE SAW CANDLES (WITH NO UV INHIBITOR) CHANGE FROM BURGUNDY TO WHITE IN ONLY 2 HOURS OF FULL SUNLIGHT.

Usually abbreviated as UV inhibitors. Candle dyes tend to be very unstable in the presence of ultraviolet light. The ultraviolet source may be from direct or indirect (reflected) sunlight, or from some fluorescent light bulbs. This is not usually a concern to the candle making hobbyist, but if you plan to sell candles you should add an ultraviolet inhibitor to reduce fading. It is important to note that these inhibitors do not eliminate fading, but they do slow it tremendously.

There are a few types on the market, with the most popular being a two-part powder that is added into the melting pot with the wax. Although ultraviolet inhibitors are relatively expensive, a small amount goes a long way. This is another product that can be obtained from full-line candle supply companies.

Release Wax

The vast majority of candle makers use a release coating on their molds, but there is an alternative—release wax. Unlike most mold release products, release wax is added to the wax mixture. It is designed to gradually build up a coating on the molds and is used in progressively smaller quantities. Although it works well, I prefer to keep my wax formulas simple and limit my use of release wax to molds that cause consistent release problems. It is melted along with the wax, and can be obtained from many full-line candle supply companies.

Wax Softeners

This category includes products that will soften wax. The two most common are petrolatum and vegetable shortening. In addition to softening the wax, they reduce shrinkage. I include them only to make you aware of them, but I personally do not like to use these products. In my experience are detrimental to candle quality, and they are messy to work with. I have also observed that many candles made with them produce excessive soot.

Mottling Compounds

Sometimes mottling is a desired appearance in a candle. There are a few ways to achieve this—mineral oil, carrier oil, scent oil, or solid mottling compound. These will be covered in greater detail later in this book.

CONTRARY TO POPULAR BELIEF, CRAYONS DO NOT MAKE GOOD CANDLE COLORANTS. THEY CONTAIN PIGMENTS THAT WILL CLOG THE WICK.

Colorants

Most waxes are supplied in a translucent or white color. In order to color them it is necessary to introduce a coloring agent. Like most candle making supplies, colorants have come a long way. All wax colorants fall into one of two categories—dyes or pigments. Oil-soluble dyes are used for most candles since these can be used in the core candle. Pigments are usually only used for external coloring since they will clog the wick and cause the candle to burn poorly.

Colorants are available in powder, liquid, and solid forms.

Oil-Soluble Dyes

Most candle coloring is done with oil-soluble dyes. These dyes are available in three main forms—solid, powder, and liquid. Dyes can be mixed to form other colors in a manner similar to paint. Unlike paint, dyes cannot be lightened and darkened using white and black. To obtain a darker color, add more dye; for a lighter color, add less. Dyes are not opaque, so they rely on thickness to provide depth of color. Because of this they do not make good colorants for overdipping candles.

Candle dyes are highly concentrated, so it is best to add a little at a time until the desired color is obtained. It is far easier to make wax a darker color than it is to lighten it when too much dye has been added.

Many candle dyes exhibit a tendency to shift color from prolonged exposure to high temperatures, so it is best not to leave colored wax on the heat source for extended periods. This is especially true for reds, browns, and greens.

Solid Form Dyes

Solid form dyes are by far the most common and easiest to use. Solid dyes are basically wax with a high concentration of dye in it. Although available in a variety of shapes, they are all used in the same way. Some solid dyes also come in flake or granule form. To use solid dyes, shave pieces off the block into the wax. If you are using a flake form dye, the shaving is usually not necessary. Solid dyes may be weighed out to make multiple batches of identical color.

ALWAYS ADD COLOR A LITTLE AT A TIME. IT IS EASY TO ADD MORE DYE, BUT IMPOSSIBLE TO REMOVE IT.

Powder Dyes

Powdered dyes are not as readily available to the average candle maker and are much more difficult to use. They are highly concentrated and will stain nearly everything on contact. The main difficulty with using them is that it requires a scale capable of weighing very tiny amounts to make repeatable colors. Another common problem is difficulty in getting them to dissolve. Although most of the time powdered dye will blend readily with the wax, all it takes is one undissolved particle of dye to stain the candle.

Liquid Dyes

Liquid dyes are exceptionally concentrated and as such they are not well suited to small lot candle production. They stain nearly everything on contact. To make repeatable colors they can be measured by drops, measuring spoons, or weight. The difficulty with using them for small batches is that it is difficult to measure less than one drop. To obtain less than one drop, mix a drop with some wax and allow to cool. This may then be handled like a solid dye. Liquid dyes tend to blend rapidly into the wax.

Pigments

In the previous section we learned that dyes do not work well in thin layers because they are not opaque. Pigments are opaque solid particles of color that are suspended in the wax. This allows us to create vibrant colors in a very thin layer of wax. The drawback to this type of coloring is that the particles will clog the wick so it is limited to external use on candles. Most crayons also contain pigments, which is why they do not work well in candles. Pigments may be blended to achieve a wide range of colors. They are blended in the same way paints are, since paints are also pigment based. Pigments are also available in metallic colors, and are the only way to obtain a true metallic color wax.

Two forms are commonly available—powdered and wax suspension. Powdered pigments are supplied as just the solid color particles. Wax suspension pigments are powdered pigments suspended in wax. Both are highly concentrated and are typically added to your wax at a rate between one percent and five percent. Of the two, wax suspension pigments are easier to use.

When using pigments it is important to stir the vat frequently. The solid particles that provide the color will settle to the bottom, and frequent stirring is needed to keep them in suspension.

Fragrances

The boom in candle popularity in recent years closely parallels the improvements in scenting them. Today's candles are scented better than ever before. When I first started making candles, a scented candle had a faint fragrance that was barely noticeable. Now candles are used to fragrance entire rooms. If you are planning to sell your candles, be aware that the largest portion of the candle market is heavily scented candles.

Candle fragrances are available in two forms—solids and oils. Although solid fragrances are the easiest to find, they are inferior to oils, and it is worth the effort to obtain fragrance oils. When shopping for fragrances, look for oils that are designed specifically for candles. Although other types of oils may work, they rarely work as well as those designed for candles.

Solid Fragrances

Solid fragrances are oils suspended in wax, usually in a block form. To use, a portion of the block is added to the wax mixture. These have been around a long time and do work to a moderate degree, but I have never had any success making heavily scented candles with solid scents.

Fragrance Oils

The best way to fragrance your candles is with fragrance oils, also known as scent oils or FO's. These are generally synthetic oils, although many have a natural component and are not totally synthetic. Look for oils designed for candle making. Those wishing to produce an all-natural candle may wish to experiment with essential oils, or EO's, but in my experience these are difficult to get good results with in candles and are best avoided. Candle scent oils are normally sold by weight, not fluid ounces. When purchasing oils bear in mind that there are few standards in the fragrance oil industry. Oils vary greatly in quality and strength. Typical fragrance oil usage is one ounce per pound of wax for a heavily scented candle.

Wicking

Nothing determines the quality of a candle more than the wick. A well made candle with the wrong size wick will often burn terribly. An entire chapter in this book is devoted to selecting the right wick, but here we will discuss the different types of wicks and their basic properties.

Flat Braided Wick

Flat braid wick is mostly used for taper and novelty candles, although it can be used interchangeably with square braided wick of equivalent wicking factor in most types of candles. Typically sized by the number of strands in the wick, *i.e.*, 12 ply, 18 ply, etc. Available in sizes from birthday candle size up to almost shoe lace size.

In use, the braiding causes the tip of the wick to curl into the hottest part of the flame. This causes the wick to be self-trimming and to burn cleaner when the proper size is used.

Square Braided Wick

Square braid wick is mostly used for pillar candles and beeswax candles of all types, although it can be used in most types of candles. The sizing system used for square braided wick is similar to that used for paint brushes with 6/0 being the smallest and #10 the largest.

As with the flat braid wick, the braiding causes the tip of the wick to curl into the hottest part of the flame, and causes the wick to be self-trimming and to burn cleaner when the proper size is used.

Cored Wick

Cored wick is square braid that has been braided around a core to increase stiffness. Common cores include zinc, paper, and cotton. At one time, lead core wick was also quite common. In light of the recent allegations about its hazards, I advise against using lead core wick should you come across any. Cored wicks are commonly used in votives, floating candles, and container candles. They are usually used with the bottom crimped into a metal wick tab, or "sustainer" as they are sometimes called. The sizing system for cored wicks is rather more arcane and technical, but the important thing to remember is that the higher the number the larger the wick. A typical wick size is 44-24-18. This would be larger than a 36-24-24 and smaller than a 44-32-18.

The core, which makes these wicks so useful for certain applications, is also the cause of their major drawback—they do not curl. Because of this they require periodic trimming when in use, and if not sized properly will develop excessive carbon buildup, often referred to as "mushrooming" or "wick mushrooms."

Miscellaneous

There are a few other materials that are useful to the candle maker.

Mold Release

As a general rule, some form of mold release is needed for most candle making. These are available in a variety of types. The most common and easy to use is silicone, which is available as either a spray or a liquid that can be wiped into the mold. Some folks advocate using spray vegetable shortening, although I find it inferior to silicone. If you are really in a pinch for a mold release, just about any vegetable oil can be used.

Wax Remover

There are a few types of wax remover on the market. These are sometimes sold as mold cleaners. They are used to dissolve wax. Some are petroleum based and some are not. Be sure to follow the directions on the bottle, as misuse may be harmful.

6

Work Area

In a perfect world, we would all have an area set aside to make our candles where we wouldn't have to worry about spills or putting away our materials after each use. In reality the vast majority of candle makers use their kitchens as their work areas. In this chapter we'll discuss basic work area set up.

Kitchen Work Area

In many ways the kitchen is an ideal place to make candles. It contains everything necessary for candle making, such as a stove, water, counters, and even a refrigerator. Kitchens are not usually carpeted, so that reduces the potential damage to the floor. They do have one major drawback; the materials cannot be left out and must be put away to make room for the kitchen's primary function—food preparation.

Although most kitchen surfaces appear to be stain resistant, candle dye is really strong and will stain most surfaces if not removed rapidly.

Although ceramic tile is not susceptible to dye stains, the tile grout is. Linoleum is also easily stained, as are many popular counter surfacing materials. Since wax is not easily removed, it is a good idea to protect all surfaces that may be exposed to drips.

- **Floor.** The floor is highly likely to get dripped on. It is a good investment to cover the floor where you are working with an inexpensive mat.

- **Counter tops.** There are a few things that may be done to protect counter tops. Cover them with a piece of aluminum foil, a mat, or even stretch cling wrap. Since molds are prone to leak when you least expect it, placing them in a shallow baking pan before pouring adds an extra measure of protection and will allow easy recovery of the wax.

- **Stovetop.** The stovetop should also be protected. Since it is a heat source, only non-flammable material such as aluminum foil can be used for this. Inexpensive aluminum burner liners can be used around the burners, with foil in the areas between the burners.

Work Shop

If you plan to spend a lot of time making candles and have the space, having a dedicated candle shop is much more convenient. Spills and drips are much less of a concern, and the equipment can be left in place after use.

- **Heat source.** If space permits and you can find an old stove, then you have a great heat source. Otherwise you will need to get a hot plate. A stove has the advantage of having an oven, which is sometimes useful for candle makers.

- **Floor.** If you put down an inexpensive floor, spillage will not be of any concern and can be periodically scraped clean. Obviously, the smoother the flooring, the easier it will be to scrape. Try to avoid working on a bare concrete floor. Concrete is porous and you will never be able to remove all the wax.

- **Counters/workbenches.** I find that the one thing my shop never seems to have enough of is counter space. When designing counters for the shop, keep in mind that narrow counters work very well. This is because it is easier to pour candles near the edge. Having two 24-inch counters takes up the same space as one 48-inch counter, but is more useful. Even more important is that the counters have a smooth surface for ease of wax removal.

• **Water.** Running water is a plus, but not necessary if it can be brought in from a nearby room.

• **Storage.** A variety of shelving is handy for keeping the workbench uncluttered. If you're like me, you will find that you can never have enough storage space. Put in as much storage area as possible.

7

Basic Candle Making Procedure

*I*n this chapter I will discuss the techniques common to most candle making, such as mixing wax formulas and melting wax. These techniques are the basis for everything that follows, so please make sure you understand before continuing to the next chapter.

Basic Steps

1. Start the water boiling. This will generally take some time, so whenever possible plan ahead. Usually two inches of water in the bottom part of your double boiler will suffice. Since we have not added the wax yet, this is no more dangerous than cooking food, and does not need to be watched closely. Check periodically to make sure the water doesn't boil off or you will have to start over.

A QUICK COLOR TEST CAN BE DONE BY POURING A SMALL AMOUNT OF WAX IN A CUP, THEN PLACING IN A FREEZER FOR FIVE MINUTES.

2. While the water is boiling, prepare the wax formula. The wax and most types of additives (those that do not need to be melted separately) are added to the melting pot. This may be placed inside the water pot at any time, but you will have to be more alert to the water level once wax is placed on the heat.

3. While the wax is melting, prepare your mold or container.

4. One the wax is completely melted, add a small amount of dye. Stir well, then test the color. Repeat this until the desired depth of color is obtained. Remember that the color of the molten wax will not even be close to the color of the finished candle. The best way to test color is to pour a small amount of wax into a cup or small mold, then place it in a freezer for five minutes. The result will be very close to the finished candle color. Note how much lighter it appears compared to the wax in the pot.

Two tablespoons of quality fragrance oil will usually provide a strong scent.

5. Once the desired color is attained, it is time to start checking the temperature. If the wax temperature is higher than your intended pouring temperature, remove it from the heat and continue to step 6. If the wax is not yet up to your intended pouring temperature, continue heating until desired pouring temperature is reached.

6. Add your fragrance (this is only for scented candles). Stir the wax thoroughly.

7. Allow the wax to settle for at least one minute. This will allow any dirt particles, undissolved dye particles, and any scent oil residues to settle to the bottom of the pot. By doing this we avoid pouring contaminants into the mold.

8. Do a final temperature check and heat or cool the wax if necessary to bring it into pouring temperature range.

9. Pour the wax into the mold or container.

10. Many types of candles will require additional steps that will be explained in the specific chapter on that type of candle.

Mixing Wax Formulas

This is not as complicated as it sounds. Most additives are added to the melting pot with the wax. Additives that have a much higher melting point than the wax need to be melted separately in a small quantity of wax. This is then added to the melting pot with the balance of the wax and stirred thoroughly. Most additives are not heat sensitive and can be added at any time.

Although not extremely sensitive to heat, many oil-soluble dyes have some degree of heat sensitivity. Many will exhibit a color shift from prolonged exposure to heat or high temperatures. This is most pronounced at temperatures over 200° F (93° C). Because of this, dye is best added near the end of the melting process. Because the dye is less sensitive to heat than fragrance, it is best to get wax to the desired color before adding fragrance.

The common misconception is that the burning of the fragrance releases the scent. Actually, fragrance works by evaporation. *Because of this, the less time the fragrance is in the molten wax, the more fragrance will be retained in the finished candle.* You will notice a heavy fragrance when making candles. While this makes candle making a pleasant way to spend some time, remember that every molecule of fragrance released while making a candle is one less molecule that will appear in the finished product.

Removing Candles From Molds

1. Once the candle has cooled, remove the wick sealer putty or plug. Hold your hand over the top of the mold and turn it upside down. Usually it will slide right out into your hand.

2. If not, grasp the wick bar and pull gently.

3. If the candle still won't come out, place the mold in a refrigerator for 20 to 30 minutes then try again.

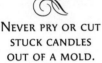

NEVER PRY OR CUT
STUCK CANDLES
OUT OF A MOLD.

4. Occasionally a candle will not want to release from the mold. In these cases place the mold in a freezer until the candle releases. First try the freezer for 5 minutes.

5. Beyond this the candle will almost always crack. Increase the time in the freezer until the candle releases.

6. If all else fails, the candle must be melted out of the mold. Do not do this with plastic molds, as it will ruin them.

7. Preheat your oven to 150° F (66° C).

8. Shut off oven.

9. Lay mold on its side in a pan or tray and place in oven.

10. The wax will melt out of the mold into the pan.

To melt wax out of a mold it must be placed on a pan or sheet with raised sides.

8

Wick Selection and Preparation

Selection

Selecting the correct wick is the most difficult part of learning to make candles. In the past I have jokingly given the following response when asked how to choose a wick: take into account the wax, additives, scent, color, mold size, time of day, phase of the moon, and the price of tea in China—then take your best guess. Eenie-meenie-miney-mo is about equally effective. With time and experience you will get an intuitive feel for it and spend less time pondering about the correct size wick.

I have used my own technique for many years without giving it much thought. In response to a lot of begging from my candle making students, I sat down and put all those things I had been doing unconsciously into a system that can be taught.

Since each component of a candle affects every other component, every change will affect the wick size needed. Accordingly, every different formula or candle size will usually require a different wick size. As mentioned in the materials chapter, it is common for materials from different suppliers to have somewhat different properties.

Choose the correct type of wick for the candle. Cored wick for containers, votives, and floating candles. Flat or square braid for molded candles and tapers. The different wick types are discussed in detail in chapter 5.

SUPPLIERS' WICK CHARTS ARE ROUGH GUIDELINES, AND YOU SHOULD NOT EXPECT THEM TO BE ACCURATE FOR YOUR WAX FORMULA.

1. Wick suppliers generally publish guidelines for their wicks in their catalog or on the packaging. Wick size guidelines usually give a range of candle diameters for that size wick using paraffin wax, for example, "3-inch to 4-inch diameter." If using a soft wax formula, this wick would be a good starting point for a 3-inch candle, or a 4-inch candle using a harder wax formula. Softer wax requires a larger wick than a harder wax in the same size mold. This will be our base size for experimentation.

2. Use the wick selected make a test candle. Allow it to cure fully—as a rule, candles should not be burned for at least twenty-four hours after making them. If you want to really be professional about it, make at least three test candles—one with the base size wick selected, one with a size larger, and one with a size smaller.

IT IS BEST TO ALLOW CANDLES TO CURE A MINIMUM OF 24 HOURS BEFORE BURNING.

Test burning with different wicks will help you determine the best size for that wax formula and mold size.

3. Burn the test candle. The bare minimum time for a test burn is one hour per inch in diameter; however, an eight-hour test burn is usually more enlightening. It is important to keep notes about the wick size, burn time, size of the melt pool, and any problems such as smoking or not staying lit.

4. Analyze the results of the test burn. Ideally we are looking for a wick that consumes wax at the same rate it is melting it. This will give us a nice burning, dripless candle that throws fragrance well. If it burns well and exhibits no problems, then you now have the correct wick for that formula in that size mold. Otherwise, refer to the following troubleshooting list:

The wick is too large causing a minimal melt pool.

- **Wick goes out**—Usually a large melt pool accompanies this. A very good indication that the wick is too small and is melting wax faster than it can wick it up.

- **Wick sputters**—Usually this is accompanied by little or no melt pool. A very good indication that the wick is too large and is wicking up wax faster than it can melt it. The flame running out of fuel causes the flickering or sputtering.

- **Candle drips**—This is usually an indication that the wick is too small. The wick needs to consume the wax at the same rate it is melting to have a dripless candle.

- **Carbon buildup on wick**—This is common with cored wicks since they do not curl into the flame. A small amount of carbon is unavoidable, but large amounts indicate that the wick is too large. This is also called mushrooming.

- **Candle produces excessive smoke**—This usually indicates that the wick is too large.

- **Wax does not melt all the way across**—This is most common in

A typical carbon mushroom. Note how some has fallen into the melt pool.

container candles. Although sometimes a smaller wick will correct it, often the problem lies with the wax. If you cannot improve the burn with a different wick, try a different wax formula.

5. Repeat steps 1 through 4 with the change in wick size indicated above. By using this process of elimination we can usually obtain a good burning candle after one or two test burnings. It is important to keep your wax formula the same throughout the testing.

Although it is not common, sometimes you will encounter a situation where none of the test candles burn well, even after several rounds of experimenting with wick sizes. This generally means that your wax formula / candle size does not match any currently available wick. In a case like this you will need to modify your formula to make it either softer or harder. The easiest way is to add a little more hardener, because the only safe way to make it softer is to use a lower melting point wax.

SOME SUPPLIERS OFFER WICK IN SMALL, MEDIUM, AND LARGE SIZES. THIS IS CONFUSING BECAUSE THERE ARE DOZENS OF SIZES OF WICK ON THE MARKET.

Summary

By following these five simple steps you will be able to determine the correct wick for just about any wax formula and any size mold or container. As you become more experienced, you will develop a knack for selecting the right wick on your first try. Keep in mind that any change in the wax formula, or even the supplier of one of the ingredients, may necessitate a change in wick size.

Beeswax Wicking

Beeswax has a higher viscosity when melted than paraffin. To put this in less technical terms, it is a thicker liquid (when melted) and requires a substantially larger wick than paraffin. When selecting wick for beeswax candles, based on a paraffin chart, add two wick sizes and start experimenting there.

Improving Burn Time

Generally a candle with the correct size wick will have the best burn time possible. If you feel it could be better, experiment with one wick size up and down.

Preparation

Most candles will not require any special wick preparation. Primed wicks are slightly easier to light, but for most candles priming is not really necessary. The exception to this is wicks used in top-up molds and containers. On these candles, primed wicks will be much easier to use, as they will stand straighter when placed. Priming also makes it easier to crimp the wick into a wick tab, which is necessary for these types of candles.

Priming

1. Melt wax. The formula intended for the candle will usually suffice. If wicks are to be used in top-up molds or containers, use of a harder formula (such as a hurricane candle formula) will stiffen the wicks more, which is helpful.

2. Cut wick into convenient lengths (one yard or meter is easily handled).

3. Grasp one end of the wick and dip the entire length (except the part you are holding) into the wax.

4. Hold in place until air bubbles stop releasing from the wick.

5. Remove from wax.

6. Although it may be held until cool, I prefer to hang it using a spring-type clothespin at each end. This allows the dipping of multiple wicks in a very short time and ensures straightness.

Adding a spring clamp or binder clip to the bottom of the primed wicks while they hang will make them cool straighter.

Tabbing

For top-up molds and containers, it will be necessary to attach the wick to a metal wick tab or *sustainer*. Wick tabs serve multiple functions. They allow the wick to stand unsupported when making the candle. They prevent the wick from leaning over in soft formulas that melt deep (votives, containers). Finally, they are supposed keep the glass from getting hot enough to crack at the bottom of the candle. I find this usually works, but not 100 percent of the time, and the occasional glass will crack regardless of a wick tab. I find this usually works, but not 100 percent, and the occasional glass will crack regardless of a wick tab when burned to the very bottom.

1. Cut primed wick to length desired.

2. Insert one end into the wick tab.

LARGER PLIERS REQUIRE LESS MUSCLE POWER TO USE

3. Crimp tab with a pair of pliers to firmly hold the wick.

9

Molded Candle Procedure— Top-Up Molds

$\mathcal{A}$lthough there is not a large selection of candle making molds that can be termed top-up molds, they are among the most popular. More candles are made in this type of mold than in any other. In this type of mold the top of the mold is the top of the finished candle. This means that the wick is inserted into the mold from the top. On molds of this type, the wick is normally placed after pouring the candle. Most votive and floating candles are made in top-up molds.

Top up molds come in a variety of shapes and materials.

Placing small molds in trays allows easier handling and spill control.

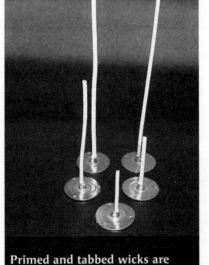

Primed and tabbed wicks are available in many sizes, and are more convenient than making them yourself.

Basic Steps— Top-Up Molds

Most molds of this type are metal, but some are plastic.

1. Prepare the wax as discussed in chapter 7.

2. Apply mold release to inside of mold.

3. Since these molds are generally small, place them in a tray. In case of leakage or spills this will make it easier to recover the wax, and will prevent a mess.

4. One primed and tabbed wick will be needed for each mold. Prepare the wicks as described in chapter 8. The mold is now ready to be poured when the wax is ready.

FRAGRANCE IS THE MOST "FRAGILE" INGREDIENT IN CANDLES AND EXPOSURE TO HEAT SHOULD BE MINIMIZED.

5. Pour the wax into the mold in a slow, steady pour. Pour to the top of the mold. On small, shallow candles, no further pouring should be necessary (skip steps 8,

Pour to the top of the mold.

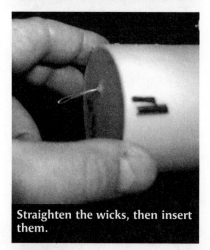

Straighten the wicks, then insert them.

Gently tug the wick upwards and to the center.

9, and 10). On larger or deeper candles, set aside the remaining wax for a later step. Do not leave it on heat as the color may shift and any scent will dissipate.

6. Allow the wax at the bottom of the mold to form a thin film of solidified wax. Straighten and place the primed and tabbed wicks in the molds. Try to get the tabs as near to the center as possible.

7. Once the wax surface starts to solidify, grasp the wicks and tug gently upwards and to the center. This may be repeated as often as necessary to keep them centered.

8. Allow the candle to cool until the wax is very firm, but the mold is still warm to the touch. The actual time this takes will vary with mold size, pouring temperature, and room temperature. You will notice a sinkhole or well caused by wax shrinkage.

9. Reheat the wax left over from the first pour to the same temperature as or slightly higher than the first pour.

10. Pour the reheated wax into the mold to fill the well caused by shrinkage. Overflow the mold slightly. This will put the joint between the two pours at the rim, where it will not be noticeable.

Allow the second pour to overflow the mold.

Always use wire cutters to trim the wick if wire core wick is used.

11. Allow the candle to cool completely.

12. Remove the candle from the mold. If the candle does not release easily from the mold, see "Removing Candles from Molds" in chapter 7.

13. Trim the wick to ¼ inch (6 mm).

Mold Maintenance

• **Care of Metal Molds—**Rust is the biggest enemy of metal molds. Immediately after use, dry thoroughly and spray or wipe with silicone. Avoid scratching or denting.

• **Care of Plastic Molds—**After use, wipe off any wax particles.

10

Molded Candle Procedure— Top-Down Molds

The vast majority of molds designed for candle making are what can be termed top-down molds. This means that candle is made upside down, with the bottom of the mold forming the top of the finished candle. On molds of this type, the wick is normally placed before pouring the candle. The wicking method described here works well; however, your molds may come with different wicking instructions.

Poking Air Holes—Dispelling the Myth

Until now the one thing most candle making books agree on is that "the first wax pour needs to have holes poked near the wick to release trapped air." What a load of manure! I don't know whether this started as a practical joke, or just a misconception. I have made hundreds of thousands of candles and have never seen an air bubble release from poking holes. Any observant candle maker will note that trapped air is always trapped against the mold surfaces; so poking holes in the candle's center will not release them.

There is a very good reason to poke holes near the wick on most candles, but it has nothing to do with air bubbles. Wax shrinks as it cools, and poking relief holes helps keep the wick straight while cooling. Holes also help the second pour to bond better with the first pour.

Basic Steps—Metal and Acrylic Molds

Most molds of this type are pillar molds. They are available in a wide variety of geometric shapes.

Assorted metal pillar molds. Similar shapes are available in acrylic.

1. Prepare the wax as discussed in chapter 7.

2. Prepare the water bath as follows (optional, but recommended for metal molds).

WATER BATHS MUST BE PREPARED BEFORE POURING BECAUSE CHANGING THE WATER LEVEL WILL LEAVE A VISIBLE MARK ON THE CANDLE.

3. Seal the mold's wick hole with mold sealer putty or a rubber plug.

4. Place a mold weight around the bottom of the mold.

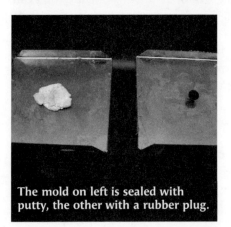

The mold on left is sealed with putty, the other with a rubber plug.

5. Hold the mold in the bottom of a pail or bucket.

6. Add water to the bucket until it reaches ½ inch from top of mold.

7. Remove the mold from the bucket.

The mold weight is wrapped around the base of the mold.

8. Make sure no water has splashed into the mold. Dry the inside of mold if necessary.

9. Remove the sealer or plug from the wick hole.

10. Make sure the outside bottom of the mold is spotlessly clean—the slightest film of wax may cause sealer failure and leakage. If you are using rubber plugs, this step is unnecessary.

Water is added while holding the mold on the bottom.

11. Apply mold release to the inside of the mold.

12. Insert the wick through the wick hole.

13. Pull the wick through and secure to the wick bar. This may be a commercially made bar, or something as simple as a pencil or metal rod. Commercial wick bars usually have a clamp built in, otherwise tie an overhand knot around the bar.

MOLDS WITHOUT BASES MUST HAVE THE WEIGHTS TAPED TO THEM IF THEY ARE TO BE PLACED IN A WATER BATH.

Tie wick to the wick bar.

If using putty the mold surface under it must be spotlessly clean.

Prepared mold ready to pour.

14. Turn the mold over and trim the wick to about 1 inch (25 mm).

15. *Option A:* Pull the wick tight and coil it in a spiral. Then cover it with a small piece of masking tape (this keeps the sealer from staining the wick). Flatten a large piece of mold sealing putty and apply covering the entire wick and masking tape.

Option B: Pull the wick tight and insert a rubber mold plug in the wick hole.

HIGH TEMPERATURES OR PROLONGED EXPOSURE TO HEAT MAY CAUSE A COLOR SHIFT IN SOME DYES.

16. Place the mold upright in a shallow pan or tray. In case of leakage or spills this will make it easier to recover the wax, and will prevent a mess.

17. Make sure the wick bar is centered. The mold is now ready to be poured when the wax is ready.

18. Pour the wax into the mold in a slow, steady pour. Pour to about ¼ inch (6 mm) from the top, then set aside the remaining

A wooden spoon can be used to tap the mold sides gently to release any clinging air bubbles.

Two or three relief holes are poked near the wick.

wax for a later step. Do not leave it on heat as the color may shift and any scent will dissipate.

19. Allow the mold to sit for 2 to 3 minutes to allow air bubbles to escape. Although usually not necessary, the sides of the mold may be tapped gently with the flat part of a wooden spoon to release trapped air bubbles.

20. Wearing heavy insulated work gloves or oven mitts, carefully transfer the mold into the water bath. The water bath must be prepared beforehand or marks will be visible from changing the water level. Although a water bath is optional, it helps speed cooling. On many metal molds it also improves the surface finish.

21. Once the wax surface starts to solidify, it is necessary to poke some relief holes near the wick. This is done with a wooden spoon handle or dowel. Do not use a metal implement inside molds, as there is a chance of scratching the sides.

22. Allow the candle to cool until fully hardened. The actual time this takes will vary with mold size, pouring temperature, and room temperature (or water bath temperature). You will notice a sinkhole or well caused by wax shrinkage.

23. Reheat the wax left over from the first pour to the same temperature or slightly higher than the first pour.

Note how the second pour is stopped below the level of the first pour.

24. Pour the reheated wax into the mold to fill the well caused by shrinkage. Stop pouring ¼ inch (6 mm) below the level of the first pour. Overflowing the first pour may ruin the finish, and will often make it difficult to remove the candle from the mold.

25. Allow the candle to cool.

26. Remove the candle from the mold. If the candle does not release easily from the mold, see "Removing Candles from Molds" in chapter 7.

27. Trim the wick from the bottom of the candle and level the base. Base leveling is common to all candles of this type, so separate instructions for this process have been included later in this chapter.

28. Trim the wick to ¼ inch (6 mm).

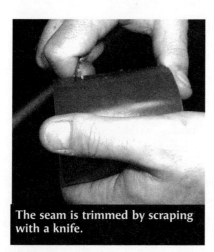

The seam is trimmed by scraping with a knife.

29. Trim the seam, if necessary. While holding the candle, scrape the seam off by holding a knife perpendicular to the seam and scraping. Do this gently, as repeated light scrapings will provide a smoother appearance. This will only need to be done with non-seamless molds.

30. Add any desired surface finish. I rarely put any type of surface finish on my candles. Most available finishes either discolor with age, smell bad when burned, or both. Should you choose to use a surface finish, follow the manufacturer's directions for use.

Mold Maintenance

Rust is the biggest enemy of metal molds. Immediately after use, dry thoroughly and spray or wipe with silicone. Avoid scratching or denting.

SOME MOLD RELEASE FORMULATIONS AND SCENT OILS MAY ATTACK PLASTIC MOLDS, SO THEY SHOULD BE TESTED ON THE OUTSIDE OF THE MOLD BEFORE USE.

Basic Steps—Two-Piece Plastic Molds

Most molds of this type are considered novelty molds. They are available in a wide variety of figurine, object, and geometric shapes. Most available molds of this type require clamps and a stand (sold separately) for use. Before the first use, a hole needs to be cut in the top of the mold for pouring the wax into—follow the manufacturer's directions on this.

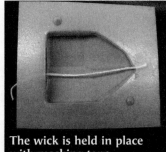

The wick is held in place with masking tape.

A commercial mold clamp is shown on the left; binder clips were used on the right and to hold the wick.

1. Prepare the wax as discussed in chapter 7.

2. Optional—spray or wipe mold with mold release. Usually not necessary on plastic molds.

3. Most molds of this type have a small channel in the bottom to hold the wick. Lay the end of the wick into the channel and hold it in place with a small piece of masking tape.

4. Pull the other end of the wick through the fill hole and either tape it in place or hold it with a binder clip (available at stationary stores).

5. Clamp the two halves of the mold together. Most two-piece molds have

CLAMPING WITH BINDER CLIPS
USUALLY WORKS BETTER THAN
MOLD CLAMPS.

some type of alignment pin, but these are generally a loose fit, so a quick visual check of the alignment should be done by holding the mold up to a bright light or looking through the pouring hole.

6. Place the mold assembly into a mold stand. Some mold stands are separate from the clamps, and some are integral with the clamps—this varies with the supplier. If you do not have a stand, the mold may be held upright in a tray of sand.

7. Place the mold upright in a shallow pan or tray. In case of leakage or spills this will make it easier to recover the wax, and will prevent a mess.

8. Make sure the wick is centered. The mold is now ready to be poured when the wax is ready.

9. Pour the wax into the mold in a slow, steady pour. Pour to the top, then set aside the remaining wax for a later step. Do not leave it on the heat as the color may shift and any scent will dissipate.

10. Allow the mold to sit for 2 to 3 minutes to allow air bubbles to escape. Although usually not necessary, the sides of the mold may be tapped gently with the flat part of a wooden spoon to release trapped air bubbles.

11. Once the wax surface starts to solidify, it is necessary to poke some relief holes near the wick. This is done with a wooden spoon handle or dowel. Do not use a metal implement inside molds, as there is a chance of scratching the sides.

12. Allow the candle to cool until fully hardened. The actual time this takes will vary with mold size, pouring temperature, and room temperature. You will notice a sinkhole or well caused by wax shrinkage.

13. Reheat the wax left over from the first pour to the same temperature as, or slightly higher temperature than the first pour.

14. Pour the reheated wax into the mold to fill the well caused by shrinkage. Stop pouring ¼ inch (6 mm) below the level of the first pour. Overflowing the first pour may ruin the finish, and will often make it difficult to remove the candle from the mold.

ALTHOUGH WAX SHRINKAGE NECESSITATES A
SECOND POUR, MOLD REMOVAL WOULD BE
DIFFICULT IF THE WAX DIDN'T SHRINK

15. Allow the candle to cool.

16. Remove the stand and clamps. Gently separate the mold halves to remove the candle. If the candle does not release easily from the mold, see "Removing Candles from Molds" in chapter 7.

17. Trim the wick from bottom of the candle and level the base. (instructions for this have been included later in this chapter).

18. Trim the wick to ¼ inch (6 mm).

19. Trim the seam. While holding the candle, scrape the seam off by holding a knife perpendicular to the seam and scraping. Do this gently, as repeated light scrapings will provide a smoother appearance.

20. Add any desired surface finish. I rarely put any type of surface finish on my candles. Most available finishes either discolor with age, smell bad when burned, or both. Should you choose to use a surface finish, follow the manufacturer's directions for use.

SEAM LINES MAY BE POL-
ISHED WITH AN OLD
NYLON STOCKING.

Mold Maintenance

After use of plastic molds, wipe off any wax particles.

Basic Steps—Silicone and Polyurethane Molds

Most molds of this type are novelty molds. They are available in a wide variety of shapes. Usually they will be a one-piece, split mold, but some are two-piece molds. These are general instructions for this type of mold—any special instructions needed will usually be supplied with the mold.

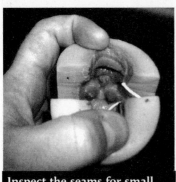

Inspect the seams for small particles of wax.

A thin piece of wire is used to thread the wick through the hole.

1. Prepare the wax as discussed in chapter 7.

2. Check to make sure all seams are clean. Small particles of wax or dirt in the seams will cause the mold to leak.

3. Apply mold release to the inside of the mold. This is optional on silicone molds, as they are self-lubricating.

4. Bend a thin piece of wire in half and insert it through the wick hole from the inside.

5. Insert the wick through the loop of wire and pull it through (this works in the same way as a needle threader). If you leave a long length of wick, you will be able to make multiple candles without rethreading the wick. As you remove a candle, the wick for the next candle is pulled through. Because the wick hole is such a tight fit, no sealer should be needed.

6. At this point you should stretch rubber bands around the mold to hold the seam closed (split molds), or put the top half in place (two-piece molds). Rubber molds are self-sealing, so no elaborate clamping is necessary.

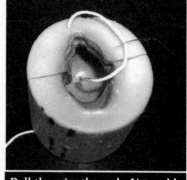

7. Secure the wick to the wick bar. This may be a commercially made bar or something as simple as a pencil or metal rod. Commercial wick bars usually have a clamp built in; otherwise tie an overhand knot around the bar.

Pull the wire through. No mold sealer should be necessary due to the tightness of the wick hole.

8. Make sure the wick bar is centered and there is no slack in the wick.

9. Place the mold upright in a shallow pan or tray. In case of leakage or spills this will make it easier to recover the wax and will prevent a mess. The mold is now ready to be poured when the wax is ready.

Split molds are held together with rubber bands.

10. Pour the wax into the mold in a slow, steady pour. Pour to the top, and then set aside the remaining wax for step 14. Do not leave it on the heat, as the color may shift and any scent will dissipate.

DO NOT USE A METAL IMPLEMENT INSIDE MOLDS, AS THERE IS A CHANCE OF SCRATCHING THE SIDES.

11. Once the wax surface starts to solidify, it is necessary to poke some relief holes near the wick. This is done with a wooden spoon handle or dowel.

12. Allow the candle to cool until fully hardened. The actual time this takes will vary with mold size, pouring temperature, and room temperature. You will notice a sinkhole or well caused by wax shrinkage.

13. Reheat the wax left over from the first pour to the same temperature or slightly higher temperature than the first pour.

14. Pour the reheated wax into the mold to fill the well caused by shrinkage.

15. Allow the candle to cool.

16. Remove the candle from the mold. Gently peel the rubber away from the candle until the candle is loose.

17. Trim the wick from the bottom of the candle and level the base (see the instructions included later in this chapter).

After removing the rubber bands, gently separate the mold to remove the candle.

18. Trim the wick to ¼ inch (6 mm).

19. Add any desired surface finish. I rarely put any type of surface finish on my candles. Most available finishes either discolor with age, smell bad when burned, or both. Should you choose to use a surface finish, follow the manufacturer's directions for use.

Mold Maintenance

Silicone is nearly indestructible, so no special care is needed other than keeping the seams clear of dirt and wax.

Basic Steps—Latex Molds

Most molds of this type are novelty molds. They are available in a wide variety of shapes, but are most commonly used for figurine candles. They are highly flexible one-piece molds that are rolled off the finished candle. Because of this, latex molds are very flimsy and need to be supported. These are general instructions for this type of mold—any special instructions needed will usually be supplied with the mold. There are other types of rubber used to make flexible molds; they are used the same way.

1. Prepare the wax as discussed in chapter 7.

2. Apply mold release to the inside of the mold. This is optional, but it will help extend the life of the mold. Be careful not to use a release formulation that will damage the latex. In general, pure silicone will not harm the latex.

3. The first time you use a latex mold it is necessary to make a wickhole. Push a large sewing needle through the mold in the area where the hole is needed.

4. Bend a thin piece of wire in half and insert it through the wick hole from the inside.

5. Insert the wick through the loop of wire and pull through (this works in the same way as a needle threader). If you leave a long length of wick, you will be able to make multiple candles without rethreading the wick. As you remove a candle, the wick for the next candle is pulled through. Because the wick hole is such a tight fit, no sealer should be needed.

A large pin or sewing needle is used to make the wick hole.

6. Secure the wick to a wick bar. This may be a commercially made bar or something as simple as a pencil or metal rod. Commercial wick bars usually have a clamp built in; otherwise tie an overhand knot around the bar.

Latex molds are not stiff enough to support their own weight, so they must be suspended.

7. Make sure the wick bar is centered and there is no slack in the wick.

8. Suspend the mold. Latex molds usually have a lip around the top. Cut a hole in a piece of corrugated cardboard large enough for the body of the mold to pass through. Place the cardboard across the top of a bucket, and then put the mold in the hole so it is supported in the bucket by its lip. The mold is now ready to be poured when the wax is ready.

9. Pour the wax into the mold in a slow, steady pour. Pour to about ¼ inch (6 mm) from the top, then set aside the remaining wax for step 14. Do not leave it on the heat, as the color may shift and any scent will dissipate.

10. Optional—the mold may now be suspended in cool water to speed cooling. This will greatly increase the life of the mold if you use stearic acid (stearic breaks down latex over time) by reducing the length of time the stearic is in contact with the mold. Prepare the water bath ahead of time according to the directions earlier in this chapter. Prepare the water bath ahead of time according to the directions earlier in this chapter. Do not fill the bucket with water while the mold is in the bucket. Changing the water level will leave a visible mark on the candle.

11. Once the wax surface starts to solidify, it is necessary to poke some relief holes near the wick. This is done with a wooden spoon handle or dowel. Do not use a metal implement inside molds, as there is a chance of damaging the mold.

12. Allow the candle to cool until fully hardened. The actual time this takes will vary with mold size, pouring temperature, and room temperature (or water bath temperature). You will notice a sinkhole or well caused by wax shrinkage.

The outside of the mold is lubricated with soapy water before peeling it off the candle.

13. Reheat the wax left over from the first pour to the same temperature, or a slightly higher temperature than the first pour.

14. Pour the reheated wax into the mold to fill the well caused by shrinkage.

15. Allow the candle to cool.

16. Wet the outside of the mold with water. Rub one drop of liquid dishwashing detergent across the entire mold surface (this will make it slippery for the next step).

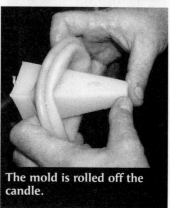

The mold is rolled off the candle.

17. Gently peel or roll the rubber away from the candle until the candle is loose.

18. Trim the wick from the bottom of candle and level the base (see the separate instructions included later in this chapter).

19. Trim the wick to ¼ inch (6 mm).

20. Add any desired surface finish. I rarely put any type of surface finish on my candles. Most available

A fine-point wire cutter simplifies trimming the wick below the wax surface of the candle.

finishes either discolor with age, smell bad when burned, or both. Should you choose to use a surface finish, follow the manufacturer's directions for use.

Mold Maintenance

After using latex molds, wash the mold thoroughly with soapy water. Rinse them off, and then dry them. Store in a cool dry place. If you plan to store them for a long time, they should be dusted lightly with talcum powder. Avoid storing in a kinked position.

Base Leveling

Base leveling is an acquired skill. Although at first it may seem difficult, after a bit of practice you will be able to do it quickly. The key to base leveling is holding the candle perpendicular to the pan—otherwise the base will either wobble or be lopsided.

Leveling a candle's base on a heated pan.

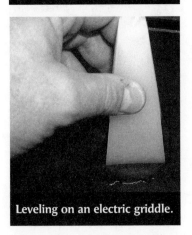

Leveling on an electric griddle.

1. Trim the wick on the candle's bottom slightly below the surface.

2. Place a baking pan atop a pot of boiling water. If you make a lot of candles an electric griddle is more convenient to use, but it is substantially more expensive.

3. Hold the candle level and press it against the pan or griddle to melt off the high spots.

4. If you need to melt off a lot of wax, it will be necessary to periodically pour off some of the melted wax (or use a spatula to push it off the griddle).

5. Avoid leveling at an angle—the base should remain parallel with the top of the candle.

Using a spatula to push excess wax off the surface of the electric griddle.

IT IS EASIEST LOOK FROM THE SIDE, NOT THE TOP, WHEN LEVELING BASES.

6. Avoid leveling with the wick protruding—this will cause a high spot in the center and the candle will wobble.

7. Once the leveling is completed, allow the candle to cool for a few minutes.

11

Container Candle Procedure

Container candles are one of the most popular types of candle. Due to their design, they can be made to melt deep and wide without fear of dripping. This enlarged melt pool helps container candles throw fragrance better than most other types of candle.

Any non-flammable object that can hold wax may be used for the container. Jars, tins, glassware, crockery, and flowerpots are the most popular. The easiest to use are those with a glossy, non-porous interior. Containers with a porous interior, such as flowerpots, must be sealed before use (see the instructions later in this chapter).

Basic Steps—Container Candles

These steps are designed mostly for clear glass containers. Opaque containers are actually easier; since you will only be able to see the top of the wax, the temperature and timing are a lot less critical.

1. Prepare the wax as discussed in chapter 7.

2. Make sure the inside of the container is clean, and that it is sealed (if necessary).

3. Most container candles will require one primed and tabbed wick. Some larger containers may need two, three, or more wicks. Prepare the wicks as described in chapter 8, or purchase them ready to use.

4. Most container candles can be poured at 185° F (85° C). If your room temperature or the jars are exceptionally cold, a higher pouring temperature may be necessary. Pour the wax into the container in a slow, steady pour. Pour to the desired level, but not to the very top. Set aside the remaining wax for step 8. Do not leave it on the heat, as the color may shift and any scent will dissipate.

5. Allow the wax at the bottom of the container to form a thin film of solidified wax. In clear containers you will see the wax changing color as it starts to harden. Straighten and place the primed and tabbed wick(s) in the container. Try to get the tabs as near to the center as possible on single wick candles, and evenly spaced on multiple wick candles.

POURING TEMPERATURE IS CLOSELY RELATED TO THE JAR OR MOLD TEMPERATURE. THE COLDER THE JAR OR MOLD, THE HOTTER YOU NEED TO POUR.

When inserting wicks, it is most important to center the tab.

6. Once the wax surface starts to solidify, grasp the wick and tug gently upwards and to the center. This may be repeated as often as necessary to keep it centered.

7. Allow the candle to cool until the wax is very firm but the container is still warm to the touch. The actual time this takes will vary with mold size, pouring temperature, and room temperature. You will notice a sinkhole or well caused by wax shrinkage.

Center the top of the wick by tugging it gently upwards and to the center.

As it cools, a sinkhole will form around the wick.

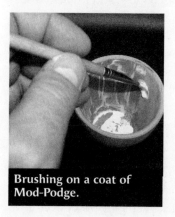

Brushing on a coat of Mod-Podge.

8. Reheat the wax left over from the first pour to the same temperature as, or a slightly higher temperature than the first pour.

9. Pour the reheated wax into the container to fill the well caused by shrinkage. Try to pour to the same level as the original pour. This will put the joint between the two pours where it will not be noticeable (it will not be noticeable on opaque containers anyway).

10. Allow the candle to cool.

11. Trim the wick to ¼ inch (6 mm).

Sealing Porous Containers

Terra-cotta flowerpots and some ceramics with unglazed interiors are porous and may pose a fire hazard if not sealed. Although it does not happen often, the molten wax may absorb into the pores, turning the entire rim into a giant wick. This will cause uncontrolled burning and should be avoided due to the fire hazard it presents. If you are using glazed (inside) ceramics or glass pots there is no need to coat the inside. Pots that are glazed outside only should be treated as unglazed. Avoid using pots of flammable material such as plastic.

My coating method of choice is to give two or more coats of Mod-Podge. This is a product readily available in most craft and art supply stores. It can also be used to put a decoupage finish on the outside of the pot as well. Since the terra cotta is porous it will

Clear silicone caulk was used to seal the drain hole.

soak in, and repeated coats should be applied until a glossy finish is obtained. Another approach is to use two coats of sodium silicate (liquid glass) to coat the pot's interior. Sodium silicate is more difficult to find and work with.

Most flowerpots have a drainage hole in the bottom. This can easily be closed off with putty or silicone. I have successfully used gray caulking putty such as Mortite, although this will sometimes melt and run from the heat as the candle burns down. Silicone caulk such as that used for fish tanks works best. Both are readily available in lumber yards or hardware stores.

Once the pot is sealed and plugged it may be treated like any other container candle. A major advantage to using containers with opaque sides is that the pouring temperature and level of the second pour are not critical. Any blemishes, air bubbles, or other defects are hidden.

Flowerpots have many advantages when properly prepared. They are inexpensive, can be painted, decaled, decoupaged, stacked, antiqued, and so on. Undecorated pots go well in a garden motif room or in the garden, and they are my container of choice for citronella candles.

Reducing Shrinkage in Container Candles

Shrinkage in container candles does more than require you to make a second pour. The wax often pulls away from the glass, leaving an air space. These air spaces are often referred to as "wet spots" because that's what they look like, although they are not truly wet. Wet spots seem to drive candle makers out of their minds, although I have never had a candle customer complain about them as long as the candle burned properly and released fragrance well.

Although it is possible to make container candles without wet spots, it is more difficult. The problem here is that the glass and your wax formula both have different "coefficients of expansion." Put simply, this means that they expand and contract at different rates. The basic scientific principle is that items expand when heated and contract when cooled. Hence fluctuations in storage temperature may cause wet spots to appear after several hours or days.

My advice is to ignore wet spots. For those who choose to ignore that advice, the following are helpful in reducing wet spots:

A classic example of a jar candle with "wet spots."

If you decide to preheat the jars, place them on a tray to make it easier to handle the hot jars.

• Use a low melt point wax. Low melt point waxes shrink less.

• Use no more scent oil than the wax can hold. Exceeding the carrying capacity of the wax will cause real wet spots as the oil leaches out of the wax.

• Pour at the lowest possible temperature. After melting and mixing the wax, allow it to cool. Pouring should be done at the point where it is about to start forming a surface film. This is somewhere between 130 and 140° F (54 and 60° C) with most wax formulas.

• Heat the jars. In order to pour at low temperatures without visible blemishes, the jars must be heated before pouring. Place the jars on a tray or pan and place in a 150° F (65° C) oven. Remove them immediately before pouring.

12

Dipped Candle Procedure

Dipped candles fall into two general categories—dipped tapers, and over-dipped candles. Both are relatively easy to master with a bit of practice.

Heat Source

Due to the repetitive dipping necessary, it is much less tiring to use a heat source set low to the ground. I find a hot plate set on cinder blocks is ideal. The ideal height for the top of the vat is one that will not require you to lift the frames above your shoulder height.

If you must use a stovetop, try to stand on a sturdy step stool or you will find dipping to be an exhausting procedure. Lifting the frames above shoulder height doubles the effort required.

Hand-Dipped Tapers

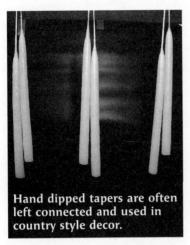

Hand dipped tapers are often left connected and used in country style decor.

At one time taper candles were commonly made in many homes. The most common material used for these was tallow—families would save every little bit of animal fat to render into tallow for candle and soap making. The rendering process was rather smelly, and the finished candles had a bad odor and smoked.

Tallow is rarely used for candle making in modern times since paraffin wax is readily available, easier to use (no rendering necessary), and more suitable in most respects. Dipping tapers is fairly simple, and is a popular project for school classes learning about Colonial life. Hand-dipped tapers are a very popular country style décor item, and they require a minimal investment in equipment.

The equipment needed for basic dipping is a dipping vat, thermometer, wire, nuts or washers, and pliers.

- Dipping vat—This may be as simple as a tall pot, or a commercially made dipping vat. The important thing to note is that it will have to be about 2 inches (50 mm) taller than the candles you plan to dip.

- Thermometer—Temperature is more critical on dipped candles than on any other type and should be monitored constantly.

- Wire—For basic dipping, a simple dipping frame can be made with a piece of stiff wire. The wire is bent into a U shape with small bends at the ends. The wick is looped over this to make two tapers at a time.

- Nuts or washers—These are tied onto the ends of the wick to weight them and keep the candles straight.

- Pliers—Used to form the wire into a dipping frame.

- Water dip container—Optional. This is required for a glossier surface effect.

Basic Taper Dipping Procedure

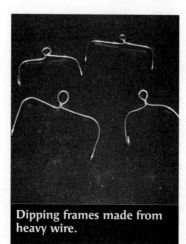

Dipping frames made from heavy wire.

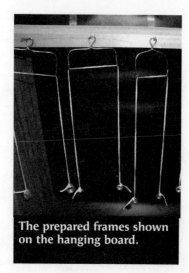

The prepared frames shown on the hanging board.

The following steps cover the basic taper dipping procedure. I highly recommend following this procedure, as it is much easier than the economy technique that follows.

1. Place the dipping vat in a pot of water and place the pot on a heat source. The quickest method for preparing large dipping vats is to melt your wax separately and pour it into the vat. The wax may be melted right in the vat, but since most vats are tall this takes much longer.

2. While the wax is melting, prepare some dipping frames. This is only necessary the first time you make tapers, as they are reusable. Generally the best quantity to work with is 6 to 8 frames.

3. Cut a length of wicking about 2½ times longer than the finished candles are to be. Next, tie a nut or washer on each end. Loop the wick over the dipping frame hooks.

4. Before proceeding it is a good idea to set up something to hang each frame from between dips. This may be as simple as a string with clothespins or a board with nails in it.

5. Once the wax is fully melted, regulate the temperature. Dipping temperature is largely a matter of personal taste, but the melting point of the wax formula also has some bearing on the necessary temperature. A bit of experimentation will be necessary, but remember—you can always remelt the experiments. I prefer a crude, rustic appearance, so I usually dip tapers at 150 to 155° F (65 to 68° C) This provides a lumpy uneven surface, and fast wax buildup. For a more formal appearance, temperatures from 155 to 165° F (68 to 74° C) will give a smoother finish.

6. The first dip is a priming dip and should be held in the vat until the wick is thoroughly soaked with wax. Air bubbles will come out of the wick as it absorbs the wax. Keep the wick in the wax until the air bubbles stop coming out of it. Allow it to cool.

7. Dip the frame in and out in one smooth motion. Dip to the same point on each dip for best results. The taper will form by itself, so no progressive dipping is necessary.

8. Hang the frame up on the device from step 4.

9. Repeat steps 7 and 8 for each frame. If you are using only one frame, allow it to harden for a short while between dips, then dip again while the candles are still warm.

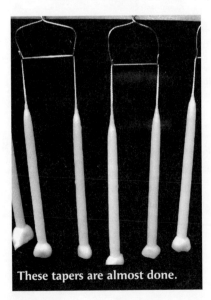

These tapers are almost done.

10. If you are using multiple frames, the first one should be ready to dip again by the time you have dipped six to eight frames.

11. Repeat steps 7 through 10 until the desired thickness is attained.

12. To obtain a smoother finish, the candle may be dipped in water immediately after the final wax dip.

13. Trim the bottom of the tapers with a razor while still warm, or with a fine-toothed saw after hardening. A band saw with an 18 tpi blade is great if you need to trim a lot of candles.

14. Return the cut-off pieces to the vat. The nuts or washers may be recovered later.

15. When you are finished, it is a good idea to pour the wax off into smaller containers such as cake pans. This will make it easier to dip different colors, and allow you to melt the wax faster for your next dipping venture.

Economy Taper Dipping Procedure

The following steps are a technique for taper dipping that allows the use of substantially less wax. This procedure is not as easy as the basic method. If you are on a tight budget it will allow you to do some dipping with minimal outlay for wax, but it requires a bit more practice to obtain good results.

1. Measure 6 to 8 inches (15 to 20 cm) from the top of the vat. Fill the dipping vat with hot water to the point measured.

2. Place the dipping vat in a pot of water and place on a heat source.

3. Melt some wax separately, and pour into vat. Do not fill past 2 inches (5 cm) from the top.

The balance of the dipping procedure is the same as the basic procedure above with one exception—the candle must be in constant motion whenever it is in the dipping vat. The bottom of the candle will extend past the wax into the water on each dip. The hot water may actually melt off some of the wax we are trying to build up if you pause mid-dip.

Over-Dipping

Over-dipping varies from taper dipping in that you start with a complete candle (referred to as a core candle from here on). Usually over-dipping is done with wax colored with pigments, not dyes. Pigments allow rapid color buildup, as they are opaque.

There are a variety of reasons for over-dipping candles. Hiding flaws, changing the color, or adding a decorative effect are the most common. This section is about over-dipping with wax. Water dipping will be covered in the projects section. The equipment needed for basic over-dipping is a dipping vat, thermometer, and a water bath container.

- Dipping vat—This may be as simple as a tall pot, or a commercially made dipping vat. The important thing to note is that it will have to be about 2 inches (50 mm) taller than the candles you plan to dip.

- Thermometer—Temperature is more critical on dipped candles than on any other type and should be monitored constantly.

- Water dip container—This helps speed the process.

Basic Over-Dipping Procedure

The following steps cover the basic over-dipping procedure. The economy technique discussed above may be substituted for a full vat of wax if necessary.

1. Make or purchase core candles. If making your own, leave a few inches of excess wick at the top as this will make them easier to grip. If using purchased candles, the wicks will usually be trimmed—these can easily be held with a pair of pliers.

2. Place the dipping vat in a pot of water and place the pot on a heat source. The quickest method for preparing large dipping vats is to melt your wax separately and pour it into the vat. The wax may be melted right in the vat, but since most vats are tall this takes much longer.

3. Prepare the water dip. This is just a second dipping vat of similar size filled with water.

4. Once the wax is fully melted, regulate the temperature. Dipping temperature is largely a matter of personal taste, but the melting point of the wax mixture also has some bearing on the necessary temperature. A bit of experimentation will be necessary, but a good starting point is 155° F (68° C).

5. Wax adheres best to warm wax, and here we are starting with fully cooled candles. The first dip is commonly called a heat soak and should be held in the vat for 30 seconds. If you are using the economy technique, the candle must be kept in constant motion, so the heat soak needs to be increased to 45 seconds.

6. After the heat soak, the candle is immediately dipped in and out of the water dip. Use a smooth, steady motion. Gently wipe off any water beads with the palm of your hand.

7. Immediately dip in and out of the wax, again using a smooth, steady motion.

8. Immediately dip in and out of the water, again using a smooth, steady motion.

9. Repeat steps 7 and 8 until the desired color or wax thickness has built up on the candle.

10. Finish with a wax dip if a matte finish is desired.

11. Finish with a water dip if a glossier finish is desired.

12. Allow the candle to cool, and then level the base.

13. When you are finished it is a good idea to pour the wax off into smaller containers such as cake pans. This will make it easier to dip different colors, and allow you to melt the wax faster for your next dipping venture.

A variety of the projects in this book use some variant of this basic procedure. The project instructions will include more details where the technique differs.

13

Non-Poured Candles

*T*he candles in this chapter require no heat, so they are well suited to working with children. Most require little or no equipment

Wax crystal candles are well suited to parties, fairs, and classrooms because they are fun, fast, and low-mess.

Wax Crystal Candles

Difficulty Rating: 0

Wax crystal candles are the absolute easiest candles to make. They require no equipment, no melting, and can be made in seconds. Because no heat is needed, they are well suited for candle making with young children or at craft fairs, where the customers may be allowed to make their own candles.

Materials

The basic materials, pre waxed wick and one or more colors of wax crystals.

- Wax crystals—One or more colors.

- Glass container—Any type of wide mouth jar, votive holder, or drinking glass may be used.

- Cored wick—Wicks should be of a suitable size for the diameter of your container. My personal preference is for zinc core, but any type of cored wick will work. If you do not wish to melt wax, you should purchase wicks that are already primed.

- Stick and spoon—Optional. A small stick and plastic spoon may be used to create designs with colored waxes if desired.

Procedure

1. Make sure the container is clean inside—any dust and dirt will be visible on the finished candle.

2. Fill the containers with wax crystals. If you plan to wrap it with cling wrap as in step 5, fill to the very top. Otherwise, stop ⅛ inch (3mm) below the rim of the container. These may be one color, or a mixture of colors. Colors may be layered horizontally, or diagonally by tilting the container. Patterns may be made with the stick.

3. Insert a primed wick into the center and trim to ⁵⁄₁₆ inch (7 mm).

4. Optional—A few drops of scent oil may be added near the wick if a scented candle is desired.

5. If it is necessary to transport the finished candle, the top may be covered with cling wrap to prevent spillage. A layer of melted wax may

also be poured over the top. Another option is to melt the top layer with a propane torch—but this is much more difficult and dangerous.

Wax crystal candles are burned like any other candle. Due to the air space between the crystals, there is substantially less wax than in a more traditional container candle. Because of this it will not burn as long or throw scent as well.

Rolled Beeswax Candles

Difficulty Rating: 1

Rolled beeswax is another simple technique well suited to working with young children. Adult supervision is necessary for the cutting steps as these require a sharp knife. Always save any scraps, as they will come in handy for smaller candles, appliqués, and other decorations.

A wide variety of shapes and sizes may be rolled from beeswax.

Materials

• Beeswax sheets—One or more colors.

• Wick—Square braided wick is normally used for beeswax. It is not necessary to prime it.

• Razor knife—A sharp hobby or utility knife.

• Straightedge—A metal ruler or yardstick works best.

• Cutting mat—To protect the work surface. This may be a commercial cutting mat, or a piece of cardboard.

• Blow dryer—If your sheets don't adhere well or are brittle, warm them slightly with a hair dryer.

• Square—*Optional.* A steel carpenter's or framer's square is quite useful for making perpendicular cuts, and will save lots of measuring.

Procedure—Pillar Candles

I'll use a pillar candle to explain the basic method, but the procedure is the same for all rolled candles.

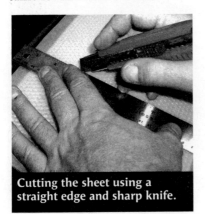

Cutting the sheet using a straight edge and sharp knife.

1. Decide on the height of the finished candle. In this example we will be making a 6-inch-high (15 cm) candle.

2. Measure and mark a 6 inch (15 cm) wide strip lengthwise on the beeswax sheet.

3. Using the straight edge, cut along the marks made in step 2.

4. If you know the length needed for the desired diameter, cut it to length. If you're not sure what length you need, make sure you keep track of your length measurement for the next time.

Form a 90-degree bend over the table edge at one end of the sheet.

5. Inspect the piece for any damages. If there are any they should be placed at the starting end in step 6. This will hide them inside the candle.

6. Place the starting edge (one of the short sides of the rectangle) slightly over a sharp table edge, and form a 90-degree bend.

7. Turn the sheet over so the bend faces up.

8. Cut a piece of wick 1 inch (25 mm) longer than the finished candle (a 7-inch or 17.5-cm wick) in this example).

9. Overlapping the ends of the sheet, lay the wick into the bend formed in step 5.

10. Press the bend over the wick to hold it in place.

11. Roll the candle starting at the wick end. Roll as tightly as possible.

12. If the sheet was not cut to length in step 4, stop rolling at the desired diameter. Mark the point at which the sheet needs to be cut. Lay the candle on its side atop the cutting mat. Unroll a bit to allow room to work and cut off the excess length using the straight-edge and razor.

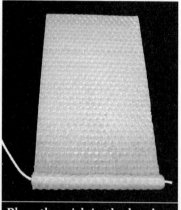

Place the wick in the bend, then start rolling.

13. If a larger diameter is desired, butt a second sheet up against the first and continue rolling.

14. Trim the wick flush on the bottom, and to ¼ inch (6 mm) on top.

Procedure—Votive Candles

Rolled votives are made in the same way, with the exception that we start with a sheet no more than 2 inches (5 cm) wide. This would be a good time to use up the scrap from the pillar example above. Votives are normally made between 1½ to 2 inches (3.7 to 5 cm) high and about 1½ inches (3.7 cm) in diameter.

Procedure—Taper Candles

Rolled tapers use the same basic procedure. The only difference is that one edge lengthwise is cut at an angle. Begin rolling at the wide end. Tapers can be made any length up to a full sheet, and in the diameter of any taper holder you want to use.

The top edge is cut at an angle when making tapers.

Layered Beeswax Candles

Difficulty Rating: 1

This technique was a favorite of my children when they were very young. It is so safe that they needed no supervision aside from having an adult cut the wick when they were done.

Materials

Complex shapes can be made very easily with this technique.

• Beeswax sheets—One or more colors.

• Wick—Square braided wick is normally used for beeswax. It is not necessary to prime it.

• Cookie cutters—A variety of shapes and sizes is useful. These will not be useable for food afterwards, so purchase some inexpensive cutters.

• Cutting mat—To protect the work surface. This may be a commercial cutting mat, or a piece of cardboard.

Procedure

The possibilities for this technique are limited only by your imagination. It is fun to watch kids making these—they approach the project with an open mind, since they generally have no preconceived notion of how the candles should look. Some good cookie cutters to start with are teddy bears, Christmas trees, pumpkins, snowmen, bunnies, and so on.

1. Use the cookie cutter to cut four or more identical shapes from the sheet. These may be all one color or a variety of colors. Always cut an even number.

A cookie cutter is used to cut the shapes.

2. Place a length of wick between two of the cutouts. Try to center it as much as possible.

3. Add additional cutouts to each side until desired thickness is reached.

4. Small scraps can be shaped and pressed in place for additional embellishment. Scraps may be kneaded; the heat of your skin will soften the wax a bit. Some suggestions for this would be eyes, buttons, bows, etc.

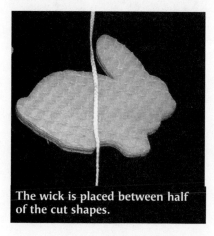

The wick is placed between half of the cut shapes.

5. Trim the wick flush on the bottom, and to ¼ inch (6 mm) on top.

6. If the candle is narrow and has trouble remaining upright, cut a base with two to three layers of wax. Mount the candle to the base.

14

Surface Effects Projects

*T*he projects in this chapter are some of the most interesting techniques for embellishing candles. I have separated them because, unlike most of the projects in this book, these procedures are applied to finished candles. Since no candle pouring is necessary, many of these projects are ideal for working with children or groups.

Asteroid Candles

Difficulty Rating: 3

This is an extremely simple technique that produces a striking candle with minimal effort. Since no heat or actual candle pouring is needed, this project may be done with anyone old enough to safely wield a hammer.

Materials

The cratered look of this candle is simple to create.

- Ball candle—A brown or gray ball candle of 3 to 5 inches (7.5 to 12.5 cm) in diameter.

- Ball peen hammer—For those unfamiliar with hand tools, a ball peen hammer has a rounded side on one end of the head.

- Towel—A folded towel or rag is needed to cushion the candle when hammering.

Procedure

1. Fold the towel and place it on a solid work surface.

2. Place the candle on the towel. This will prevent the work surface from marring the candle while hammering. One hand must hold the candle while hammering.

3. Holding the hammer in the opposite hand, strike the candle with the ball side of the hammerhead.

The ball end of the hammer is used to strike the candle.

4. Repeat until the candle is completely covered with "craters," turning the candle as needed.

Variations

The instructions above are for a basic asteroid candle. The following techniques offer ways to vary the appearance of the finished candle:

Patterns

Instead of randomly making hammer impressions, you may place them in a pattern. If you desire to do this, hold the hammer in position and strike it with a mallet or block of wood.

Crater Depth

For a more realistic looking asteroid, vary the depth of the craters by varying the strength of your blows.

Rub 'N Buff

This is a waxy product that may be applied with a soft cloth or fingertip to highlight the texture once all hammering is complete.

Water Dipped Candles

Difficulty Rating: 4

The patterns created by hot water dipping are totally random, and no two will be alike.

Hot-water dipping is interesting because a wide variety of surface finishes may be achieved. The actual texture obtained will vary depending mostly on water temperature and dipping speed.

Since this process uses finished candles, it is not necessary to make them yourself. If you do make them yourself, leave at least 6 inches (15 cm) of wick on top for ease of dipping.

Materials

In addition to the basic materials you will need:

• Candles—Most types of molded candles work well with this technique.

• Water vat—A container that is at least 2 to 3 inches (5 to 7.5 cm) taller than the candles you plan to dip.

• Pliers—If you are using candles that you did not make specifically for dipping, pliers will be handy for holding the wick while dipping.

Procedure

1. Fill the water vat and place it on a heat source. Do not fill it to the top since the candles will displace water when dipping. Please note that the water should not be allowed to boil.

2. Prepare the candles for dipping. If you made the candles with dipping in mind, tie a loop large enough to fit a finger in near the end of the wick. If the wick is too short to make a loop, it may be held in a pair of pliers.

3. Once the water is hot, make a test dip. Dip the candle in and out with one steady motion.

4. Examine the candle. If no texture appears on the candle, the water is probably not hot enough.

5. Repeat dipping until the desired texture is achieved.

6. Trim the wick to ¼ inch (6 mm).

Variations

The instructions above are for a basic hot-water dipped candle. The following will all make a visible difference on the finished candle:

Temperature
Different temperature water produces different effects.

Holding
Hold the candle in the water.

Dipping Speed
Vary the speed that the candle is inserted and removed from the water.

Wax Buildup

With very hot water, wax will melt completely off the candle and float on the surface. This may be picked up on successive dips in a random pattern. You must dip fast or you will just melt more wax off, instead of building it up.

Clean Water Surface

Excess wax buildup on the water surface may be removed by folding up a sheet of clean newspaper and skimming the wax off the surface with it.

Spinning

Spinning or twirling the candle while dipping will affect the pattern.

Rub 'N Buff

This is a waxy product which may be applied with a soft cloth or fingertip to highlight the texture once all dipping is complete.

Marbled Candles

This technique, like the last one, uses hot water. Since this process uses finished candles, it is not necessary to make them yourself. If you do make them yourself, allow at least 6 inches (15 cm) of wick on top for ease of dipping.

The diversity possible with this technique is amazing.

Materials

In addition to the basic materials you will need:

- Candles—Most types of molded candles work with this technique. Candles with a slightly domed, pointed, or round top work a bit better than flat-topped candles.

• Water vat—A container that is at least 2 to 3 inches (5 to 7.5 cm) taller than the candles you plan to dip.

• Dye—Wax-based blocks of candle dye are most suitable.

• Toothpicks—For stirring the dye.

• Newspaper—For cleaning the water of dye between colors.

• Pliers—If you are using candles that you did not make specifically for dipping, a pair of pliers will be handy for holding the wick while dipping.

Procedure

1. Fill the water vat and place it on a heat source. Do not fill it to the top since the candles will displace water when dipping. Please note that the water should not be allowed to boil.

2. Prepare the candles for dipping. If you made the candles with dipping in mind, tie a loop large enough to fit a finger in near the end of the wick. If the wick is too short to make a loop, it may be held in a pair of pliers.

The floating dye is stirred to create an interesting pattern before dipping.

3. Once the water is hot, drop in a few small shavings from the dye block. Allow the dye to melt. It will float on the water surface.

4. Use a toothpick to stir the dye. Make sure to break up any large concentrations.

5. Dip the candle in and out quickly. Do not hold the candle in the vat, as this will start melting it.

6. Trim wick to ¼ inch (6 mm) if necessary.

Variations

The instructions above are for a basic marbled candle. The following variants may be used to vary the appearance:

Spinning

Spinning the candle by twirling the wick as you dip will impart a swirl pattern.

Multicolor

Do not put more than one color in the vat at one time—they will blend. To add more than one color, dip candles into one color at a time. Any dye on the water surface must be removed before starting the next color. You can do this by folding up a sheet of clean newspaper and skimming the wax off the surface with it. It is usually best to start with the lightest color and finish with the darkest color.

Snowball Candle

Difficulty Rating: 5

This candle is a wintertime favorite.

This technique introduces whipped wax. A large variety of interesting candles may be created with whipped wax. This project uses finished candles; it is not necessary to make them yourself. If you do make them yourself, allow at least 1 inch (2.5 cm) of wick on top for ease of use.

Materials

In addition to the basic materials you will need:

- Candles—Ball candles of any diameter, scented or unscented.

- Whisk or hand blender—To whip the wax. Note that it will no longer be usable for food preparation.

- Fork—A normal dinner fork is used to apply the whipped wax.

IF YOU PLAN TO MAKE A LOT OF WHIPPED WAX PROJECTS, AN INEXPENSIVE ELECTRIC HAND MIXER WILL MAKE LIFE EASIER.

Formula

Any basic pillar candle formula may be used. The use of an opaquing additive such as Vybar or Stearic will make the whipped wax white.

Procedure

Air is whipped into the wax using a blender or whisk.

Apply the whipped wax with a dabbing motion.

1. Prepare the wax as for a basic pillar candle.

2. Once the wax is melted, remove it from the heat.

3. While cooling, periodically whip with the whisk or blender.

4. Continue whipping the wax until it has a consistency that is easily picked up on the fork. At this point it will have a texture similar to cooked oatmeal.

5. Use the fork to apply the whipped wax to the bottom half of the candle. A dabbing motion (up and down) works better than a smearing motion (left and right).

6. Once the bottom half is covered, set the candle down on a clean smooth surface.

7. Apply whipped wax to the upper half of the candle.

8. Allow the wax to cool.

9. Trim the wick to ¼ inch (6 mm) if necessary.

Cake Candles

Difficulty Rating: 5

Cake candles are very popular.

Cake candles have been very popular since the mid-1990s. Cake candles are a variant use for whipped wax.

Materials

The same materials used for snowball candles will suffice. This technique is normally used with a heavily scented round or square core candle.

Procedure

The procedure is the same as for snowball candles, using the whipped wax as "frosting" for the core candle.

Variations

Different Color Core

The core candle wax may be a different color than the whipped wax. Some folks use a knife or cookie cutter while the whipped wax is still soft to create windows that allow the core to show through.

Grubby or Grunge Candle

Use very dark colors and top with a wash of dark candle stain.

Candle Stain

Difficulty Rating: 4

Staining is most effective on textured candles.

Candle dye may be dissolved in mineral spirits to create a stain. This may be used for a variety of purposes, such as increasing contrast on textured candles. *Warning*—this procedure is best done in a well ventilated area.

Materials

- Oil-Soluble candle dye—Some dyes dissolve better than others, so if you have difficulty, try a different type.

- Mineral spirits—From the hardware or paint store.

- Metal or glass cup—I use metal votive cups for small quantities and glass jars for mixing larger quantities.

Procedure

1. Dissolve the dye in some mineral spirits. This may take some time, so I usually prepare the stain a day or two before needed.

2. Use a soft brush to apply the stain to the candle.

3. Allow the stain to dry overnight.

4. If more contrast is desired, buff the candle surface with a soft cloth.

15

Appliqué Candles

*A*dding wax appliqués easily embellishes plain candles. Since this is the simplest way to progress beyond plain candles, I have devoted this entire chapter to it. There are a variety of ways to create unique appliqué candles, and they are discussed below in order of difficulty.

Since appliqués are applied to finished candles, some of the following techniques are easily adaptable for working with young children.

Beeswax Appliqué Candles

Difficulty Rating: 1

Beeswax is the easiest type of appliqué to work with because it can be purchased in sheet form, it is moderately sticky, and it is very flexible. This flexibility simplifies application on curved surfaces.

Materials

This is the easiest type of appliqué candle to make.

- Beeswax sheets—One or more colors. Smooth or honeycomb sheets may be used.

- Knife—A sharp #11 hobby knife works best.

- Cookie cutters—May be used to easily cut repetitive shapes.

- Cutting surface—A commercial cutting board or a thick piece of cardboard will work.

- Blow dryer—An electric hair dryer or temperature-adjustable heat gun.

- Tacky wax—Optional, but useful if you have trouble adhering the appliqués.

- Ice pick—Optional. Useful for "spot welding" the appliqué to the candle. It must have a wood handle. Not recommended when working with children.

Procedure

This technique may be done with a cookie cutter; custom shapes may be cut with a knife.

1. If you are using a cookie cutter, skip to step 6.

2. Draw your appliqué design on heavy paper or thin cardboard to create a pattern.

3. Cut out the pattern using a knife or scissors.

4. Place a beeswax sheet on the cutting surface.

5. Position the pattern, and cut around it with a sharp knife.

6. If you are using a cookie cutter, press it into the sheet to make a cutout.

7. Repeat the above steps until the desired number of appliqués has been made.

8. Soften an appliqué by placing it face down on the cardboard and using the blow dryer to heat it. Keep the dryer moving and avoid making the appliqué too hot, as it will melt.

9. Once the appliqué is soft it will adhere better and can now be positioned on the candle. Gently press it in place.

10. Optional—For better adhesion, a thin layer of tacky wax may be applied to the back of the appliqué before placing it on the candle instead of heating it.

11. Optional—For maximum adhesion, the appliqué may be "welded" on by touching a heated ice pick to the seam where the edge of the appliqué touches the candle.

Flat Paraffin Appliqué Candles

Flat paraffin appliqués can be shaped with a cookie cutter or knife.

Difficulty Rating: 2

Paraffin appliqué candles are made in the same way as above, but are slightly more difficult. Paraffin sheets are not commercially available, so they must be made before they can be used. Since pure paraffin is not as flexible as beeswax, additives must be used to allow it to flex to the contours of the candle.

Materials

In addition to the tools used for beeswax appliqué candles, the following will be needed:

• Cookie sheet—One with raised edges.

• Waxed paper

• Paraffin wax—A relatively high melt point wax is best. Try to use wax with a melt point in the range of 140 to 145° F (60 to 63° C).

• Tacky wax—Or additive of preference.

• Dye or pigment—Since the appliqué is on the outside of the candle, wick clogging from pigment should not be a problem.

Formula

This is my preferred recipe for wax sheets. Any sculpting wax formula should work. I find this formula is moderately flexible, yet cools to a fairly hard finish.

1 pound 140° F (60° C) melt point paraffin wax
4.8 ounces of tacky wax. This is 30%. The percentage may be increased if you wish a more flexible formula, sacrificing finish hardness. If you decrease this amount a harder finish will be obtained, but the wax will be less flexible.
Dye or pigment to obtain the desired color

Procedure

This technique may be done with a cookie cutter; custom shapes may be cut with a knife.

1. Place the wax mixture on heat.

2. While the wax is melting prepare the cookie sheet by lining it with waxed paper, overlapping the sides. Fold the paper in the corners, so that it lies as flat as possible.

3. Place the cookie sheet on a level surface.

4. Dye the wax to the desired color.

5. The pouring temperature is not critical, but somewhere in the range of 170 to 180° F (77 to 82° C) is satisfactory.

6. Slowly pour the wax into one corner of the cookie sheet. If the sheet is level, it will flow all the way across. Any thickness sheet may be made, but sheets ⅛ inch or less are easiest to work with.

7. As soon as the wax is firm to the touch, cut your appliqués.

8. Adhere your appliqués with tacky wax or a heated ice pick.

Reheating

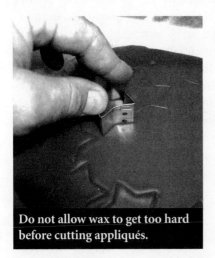

Do not allow wax to get too hard before cutting appliqués.

Unlike beeswax, paraffin will lose it flexibility when it cools. The following techniques can be used to reheat sheets or appliqués that cool before you have a chance to use them. The exact times needed will vary with the hardness of your wax formula.

Small pieces may be placed in hot water until they soften enough to bend or cut.

Larger pieces or full sheets may be softened on an electric heating pad. Place 4 to 6 layers of paper towels on the heating pad. Cover these with a sheet of aluminum foil. Place the wax sheet on the foil to soften. Some people find it useful to place the lid of a paper carton over the top to trap the heat. This allows the sheet to warm from both sides.

Another method that can be used for large pieces and sheets is to place them in a preheated oven. Set the oven to about 150° F (63° C). Cover a cookie sheet with aluminum foil and place the wax sheet on top. Place it in the oven until it is soft. *Important*—To prevent any possible chance of the wax melting into the oven, always use a cookie sheet with raised sides, not a flat sheet.

Three-Dimensional Appliqué Candles

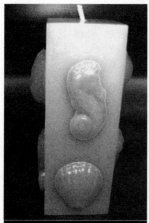

Three-dimensional appliqués can add a lot of visual interest to plain candles.

Difficulty Rating: 4

Three-dimensional appliqué candles can be extremely interesting. By combining the products of two or more molds, this technique allows us to create a huge variety of candles. The higher difficulty rating is for applying these to curved surfaces—they only rate a difficulty of 2 if applying them to flat surfaces.

The appliqués are made in open-top molds (also referred to as single-sided or flat molds). This type of mold is most commonly available in plastic, although there are some commercially available rubber molds as well. In addition to molds made specifically for candles, molds made for chocolate (candy), soap, and plaster are often usable for appliqué candles. Although there are relatively few open-top candle molds available, there are thousands of chocolate molds in almost any shape you can imagine. *Important*—when using plastic chocolate molds, the pouring temperature must not exceed 165° F (74° C) or it will damage the mold.

Materials

In addition to the tools used for beeswax appliqué candles, the following will be needed:

• Open-top mold

• Tray of sand

• Paraffin wax—A relatively high melt point wax is best. Try to use wax with a melt point in the range of 140 to 145° F (60° to 63° C)

• Vybar 103—Or additive of your preference.

• Dye or pigment—Since the appliqué is on the outside of the candle, wick clogging from pigment should not be a problem.

Formula

This is my preferred recipe for three-dimensional appliqués. Any of the pillar candle formulas in chapter 21 may be substituted. I find this formula is hard, and it has good opaque color properties.

> *1 pound 140° F (60° C) melt point paraffin wax*
> *1 level teaspoon Vybar 103*
> *Dye or pigment to the desired color*

Procedure—Plastic Molds

This technique may be done with most types of open-topped molds. If you are using rubber molds see also "Procedure—Rubber Molds."

1. Place the wax mixture on heat.

2. While the wax is melting, prepare the mold by placing it in a bed of sand. This will help keep the mold level—especially when working with irregularly shaped molds.

3. Bring the wax to the desired pouring temperature.

4. Dye the wax to desired color.

The mold is supported in a bed of sand.

5. Pour the wax into the molds. Try not to overflow the mold cavities, and you will reduce the amount of trimming required later.

6. Allow the appliqués to cool fully.

7. Remove the appliqués from the mold. Use a sharp knife to trim the edges if needed. If you are using the appliqués on a flat-sided candle, skip to step 10.

8. To use the appliqués on a curved surface, they must have the same curvature on the back. Place a metal mold similar in size to your finished candle in a preheated oven—150° F (66° C). Place it on a cookie sheet for safety.

9. Remove the preheated mold from the oven. Immediately press the appliqué against the curvature of the mold. Pay extra attention to the design of the appliqué in relation to the curvature. This is not to avoid losing detail, but to ensure correct orientation to the curvature. For example, a heart that is applied to the heated mold in the wrong direction may not align properly with the intended orientation of the heart top—say, at right angles to the axis of the candle.

10. Adhere the appliqué to the candle with tacky wax or a heated ice pick.

Procedure—Rubber Molds

Open-top rubber molds simplify the procedure since they are flexible enough to remove appliqués before they fully harden.

1. Place the wax mixture on heat.

2. Bring the wax to the desired pouring temperature.

3. Dye the wax to the desired color.

4. Pour the wax into the mold. Try not to overflow the mold cavities, as that will increase the amount of trimming required later.

5. Once the wax has cooled enough to be relatively firm yet still flexible, it is time to remove it from the mold. Hold the mold upside down over a clean pan and flex the mold. If the wax has cooled enough, the appliqués should come out easily; otherwise wait a few minutes and try again. The exact time needed will vary with the size of the mold, pouring temperature, and room temperature.

6. As soon as the appliqués are removed from the mold, use a sharp knife to trim the edges if needed.

7. Press the appliqué in place on the candle.

8. Allow the appliqué to cool in the desired curvature.

9. Adhere the appliqué to the candle with tacky wax or a heated ice pick.

16

Poured Candles—
Beginner Projects

F have selected these projects for their simplicity. All are good examples of very basic projects that will acquaint you with the skills needed for similar, more advanced projects.

Most novice candle makers try too many techniques at once. This is understandable since it is so much fun, but please avoid this temptation. My experience has shown that candle makers who master one technique before moving on to the next actually progress faster than those who try to "do it all at once."

Votive Candles

Votives release fragrance well when made right.

Difficulty Rating: 4

Votives are the most popular type of poured candle, so it is no surprise that they are also the type of candle most beginners start with. They are quick and easy to make, plus there is the added benefit that votive molds are inexpensive.

The most popular votive molds are the 15-hour metal votive cups. The top-up procedure is used for these. When made properly they will burn for about 15 hours. If you require a decorative top or a smaller votive it is necessary to use a plastic or rubber mold and the top-down procedure. The average burn time on these is 8 to 10 hours.

The procedure outlined below is for metal votive cups. If you are using a top down votive mold, the procedure is the same as discussed in chapter 10.

Materials

- Molds—One or more.

- Wick—Primed and tabbed cored wick. They may be purchased already primed and tabbed, or you can prepare them yourself.

- Paraffin wax—A relatively low melt point wax is best. Try to use wax with a melt point in the range of 128 to 135° F (53 to 57° C).

- Vybar 260—Or your choice of additives.

- Scent oil—Optional.

- Dye—Optional.

- Pan or tray—Optional, but highly recommended. Placing the molds in a pan will contain spills and allow you to easily reuse spilled wax.

Formula

This is my preferred recipe for votives. Chapter 21 contains some alternates.

1 pound 130° F melt point paraffin wax
1 level teaspoon Vybar 260.
1 ounce scent oil—The amount required will vary with the quality of the oil and how strongly scented you want the candles to be. One ounce is fairly typical.
Dye—As much as needed to achieve the desired color.

Procedure

The first couple of times that you make votives, it is easier to use a light color. This will allow you to see when the wick is ready to insert.

1. While the wax is melting, prepare the wicks (prime and tab them). If you purchase primed and tabbed wicks, skip this step.

2. Melt the wax. Add Vybar 260.

3. Coat your molds with mold release.

4. Place the molds on a pan or tray.

5. Once the wax is fully melted, add dye.

6. Test the color of your wax and add more dye as needed.

7. Bring the temperature to 185 to 190° F (85 to 88° C).

8. Add scent oil. Stir well.

9. Allow the wax to settle for 2 to 3 minutes. This will allow any residue, dirt, or undissolved dye particles to sink to the bottom of the pouring pot.

10. Pour the wax into your molds to the very top and allow them to overflow slightly. This will put the seam between the two pours at the rim, where it is less noticeable.

11. Set the leftover wax aside for a later step. Do not leave it on the heat source.

12. Allow the candles to cool until a thin film of solidified wax is on the bottom. This is hard to describe, but you will see a noticeable difference as the wax cools.

13. Straighten the wicks and gently place them in the molds. Try to center the tabs. Pay extra attention to the "feel" of the tab hitting bottom, because in dark wax you will have to rely on this "feel" to know if the candles are ready for wicks yet.

14. Allow the candles to cool for 30 more minutes. Give the wicks a gentle tug to the center and upwards. This will help keep them centered and straight. Repeat this step as often as necessary.

15. The candles are ready for their second pour once the surface is firm to the touch, but the mold must still be warm to prevent air bubbles from forming. The actual time will vary (mostly due to room temperature). With a bit of practice, you will be able to time your second pour perfectly. The leftover wax from step 11 will definitely need to be reheated as by this point it will have solidified.

16. The second pour should be made at the same or slightly higher temperature as the first pour, so you'll have to reheat the wax before pouring. Once again pour until the wax overflows the mold.

17. Allow the candle to cool.

18. Once the wax is fully cooled, the candles should come out of the molds quite easily. If they do not, refer to the section on removing candles from molds in chapter 7.

19. Trim the wicks to ¼ inch (6 mm)

Alternate Votive Method

In recent years a product has been introduced that greatly simplifies votive making. They are marketed as auto wick pins, or just wick pins. These are

Auto wick pins simplify votive making.

basically a steel pin welded to a steel disk. The disc is the same size as the bottom of the mold, so they are self centering. In use they are placed into the mold before pouring, and removed once the candle is removed from the mold. To use auto wick pins, modify the basic votive instructions above as follows:

3. Check the autowick pins for straightness, then insert them in your molds before coating the molds with mold release.

7. Pour the wax at 190 to 195° F (88 to 91° C)

12–14. Skip these steps.

18. Add to this step the pin removal. Grasp the votive upside down and press the pin against the table. Remove the pin.

19. Insert a tabbed wick through the hole left by the auto wick pin before trimming the wick.

Floating Candles

Difficulty Rating: 3

Floating candles, or "floaters" as they are commonly called, are simple to make and are very popular. Because they are floated in water, they are much safer to use than other types of candles. The elegance of candles floating in water makes them very popular for wedding and banquet centerpieces.

A common misconception is that special wax needs to be used for floating candles. This is not true—all wax floats, since it is lighter than water. Suitability for use as a floater is determined by the mold—if the candle is wider than it is deep, it will float upright. If not, it will float on its side.

The most popular floater molds are small tart pans. The top-up procedure is used for these. When made properly they will burn for about 3 to 4 hours. The procedure outlined below is for small floating candles, which only require one

Floaters are popular for banquets, but are great for everyday use as well.

wick. If you are making larger floaters, it is often necessary to use multiple wicks, but the procedure is the same.

Materials

• Molds—One or more.

• Wick—Primed and tabbed cored wick. They may be purchased already primed and tabbed, or you can prepare them yourself.

• Paraffin wax—A relatively high melt point wax is best. Try to use wax with a melt point in the range of 140 to 145° F (60 to 63° C).

• Vybar 103—Or your choice of additives.

• Scent oil—Optional.

• Dye—Optional.

• Pan or tray—Optional, but highly recommended. Placing the molds in a pan will contain spills and allow you to easily reuse spilled wax.

Formula

This is my preferred recipe for floating candles. Chapter 21 contains some alternates. A fairly hard formula is desirable, as it will extend burn time.

1 pound 140° F (60° C) melt point paraffin wax.

2 level teaspoons Vybar 103.

1 ounce scent oil—Optional. The amount required will vary with the quality of the oil and how strongly scented you want the candles to be. One ounce is fairly typical.

Dye—As much as needed to attain the desired color.

Procedure

The first couple of times that you make floating candles, it is easier to use a light color. This will allow you to see when the wick is ready to insert.

1. While the wax is melting, prepare the wicks (prime and tab them). If you purchase primed and tabbed wicks, skip this step.

2. Melt the wax. Add Vybar 103 (or hardener of your preference).

3. Coat your molds with mold release.

4. Place the molds on a pan or tray.

5. Once the wax is fully melted, add dye.

6. Test the color and add more dye as needed.

7. Bring the wax temperature to 185 to 190° F (85 to 88° C).

8. Add scent oil. Stir well.

9. Allow the wax to settle for 2 to 3 minutes. This will allow any residue, dirt, or undissolved dye particles to sink to the bottom of the pouring pot.

10. Pour the wax into your molds to the very top, allowing them to overflow slightly.

11. Set the leftover wax aside for a second pour, if needed. Do not leave it on the heat source. A second pour will usually only be necessary on very large or deep floating candles.

12. Allow the candles to cool until a thin film of solidified wax is on the bottom. This is hard to describe, but you will see a noticeable difference as the wax cools. This is critical on floating candles, as water will enter from the bottom of the candle if the wick and tab are not totally covered by wax on the bottom.

13. Straighten the wicks and gently place them in the molds. Try to center the tabs. Pay extra attention to the "feel" of the tab hitting bottom, because in dark wax you will have to rely on this "feel" to know if the candles are ready for wicks yet.

14. Before the wax surface starts to film over, make sure the wicks are centered and straight.

15. A second pour is only needed on large or deep candles. The candles are ready for their second pour once the surface is firm to the touch, but the mold must still be warm to prevent air bubbles from forming. The actual time will vary (mostly due to room temperature). With a bit of practice, you will be able to time the second pour perfectly. It should be made at the same or slightly higher temperature as the first pour, so the wax may need to be reheated. Once again pour until the wax overflows the mold.

16. Allow the candles to cool.

17. Once the wax is fully cooled, the candles should come out of the molds quite easily. If they do not, refer to the section on removing candles from molds in chapter 7.

18. Trim the wick to ¼ inch (6 mm).

Tea Light Candles

Difficulty Rating: 3

Tea lights are simple to make.

Tea light candles are also simple to make. Unscented tea lights are usually manufactured in huge quantities on mass-production machinery. Because of this, it is usually cheaper to buy unscented tea lights than it is to make them. Scented or colored tea lights are not usually mass-produced, so it is necessary to hand pour these.

The formula and procedure for tea lights is identical to floating candles with the exception of using tea light cups instead of molds.

Container Candles

Difficulty Rating: 3

Container candles are relatively simple to make, and have the added benefit of not requiring a mold.

Materials

• Container—One or more.

• Wick—Cored wick. Wicks should be primed and tabbed.

• Wax—A blended container wax is easiest.

• Scent oil—Optional.

• Dye—Optional.

A variety of non flammable containers may be used for candles.

Formula

This is my preferred recipe for container candles. Chapter 21 contains some alternates.

> *1 pound blended container wax.*
> *1 ounce of scent oil—The amount required will vary with the quality of the oil and how strongly scented you want the candles to be. One ounce is fairly typical.*
> *Dye—As much as needed to achieve the desired color.*

Wick Selection

As with any other type of candle, some experimentation may be needed to find the correct wick for each mold size/wax formula combination. Ideally we are looking for a nice flame, a deep melt pool (approximately ⅜ inch to ½ inch deep), and full melt across the entire jar diameter.

For safety purposes, a cored wick is best. This should be crimped into a metal tab (wick sustainer). This combination of cored wick and sustainer will greatly reduce the chances of cracking the container due to overheating since they will help keep the flame away from the glass.

Procedure

The procedure outlined in chapter 11 should be followed. If you find that you are having problems with excessive wax shrinkage or poor scent throw, the following alternate procedure should be tried. I personally do not feel the additional work required for this alternate technique is worth the effort, but many candle makers swear by it.

Alternate Procedure

This procedure allows pouring at a substantially lower temperature, which will reduce wax shrinkage. The more wax is heated, the more it expands; so conversely, the more it cools, the more it shrinks. By pouring at a lower temperature, we are reducing the shrinkage as much as possible.

The lower pouring temperature will also reduce the evaporation of scent oil, leaving the finished candle with a bit more scent. Preheating the containers allows use of a much lower pouring temperature without trapping unsightly air bubbles.

This technique is usually used only for clear glass containers, since opaque containers can be poured at lower temperatures with no extra steps (the trapped air will not be visible in opaque containers).

1. Prepare the wax as discussed in chapter 7.

2. Make sure the inside of the container is clean.

3. Most container candles will require one primed and tabbed wick. Some larger containers may need 2, 3, or more wicks. Prepare the wicks as described in chapter 8.

4. Preheat an oven to 150 to 160° F (65 to 71° C). Note that a higher temperature may be needed if an exceptionally cool pouring temperature is used.

5. Place the containers in the oven for approximately 30 minutes. If you are using jars, remove the lids first. To make it easier to handle the hot glass, place the containers on a pan or sheet.

6. Once the wax is fully melted, stir in dye. Remove the wax from the heat.

7. Monitor the wax temperature. When the temperature drops to 150° F (65° C), add the scent oil and stir thoroughly.

8. Allow the wax to continue cooling until the desired pouring temperature is reached. The exact pouring temperature with this technique is largely a matter of personal preference. I have used this technique at temperatures as low as 115° F (45° C) with some waxes, but for your initial experiments I suggest a pouring temperature of 135° F (57° C).

9. Once the desired pouring temperature is reached, remove the containers from the oven. Use potholders or oven mitts as the glass and trays will be hot.

10. Immediately pour the wax into the containers in a slow steady pour. Pour to the desired level, but not to the very top. Set aside the remaining wax for a second pour. Do not leave it on the heat, as the color may shift and any scent will dissipate.

At this point the procedure is the same as the basic procedure starting with step 5, so I won't repeat it here.

Plain Molded Candles

Difficulty Rating: 4

Plain molded candles are the basic candles that most of the intermediate and advanced projects are based on. Use the following information with the procedure from chapter 10 for the type of mold you wish to use.

Materials

• Molds—One or more.

• Wick—Square or flat braid wick. Wick may be primed, but that is optional.

• Paraffin wax—A relatively high melt point wax is best. Try to use wax with a melt point in the range of 140 to 145° F (60 to 63° C).

• Vybar 103—Or your choice of additives.

• Scent oil—Optional.

• Dye—Optional.

Plain pillar candles have a simple elegance.

• Water bath—Optional, but recommended for metal molds.

• Pan or Tray—Optional, but highly recommended. Placing the molds in a pan will contain spills and allow you to easily reuse spilled wax.

Formula

This is my preferred recipe for basic molded candles. Chapter 21 contains some alternates.

1 pound 140° F (60° C) melt point paraffin wax.
1 level teaspoon Vybar 103.
1 ounce scent oil—The amount required will vary with the quality of the oil and how strongly scented you want the candles to be. One ounce is fairly typical.
Dye—As much as needed to achieve the desired color.

Wick Selection

As with any other type of candle, some experimentation may be needed to find the correct wick for each mold size/wax formula combination. Ideally we are looking for a nice flame, medium-depth melt pool (approximately ¼ inch deep), and no running or dripping of the melted wax. Essentially this means that the wick will melt the wax at the same rate it consumes it.

It is important to note that some candle shapes cannot be made totally dripless. For candles with extreme tapers or odd shapes, a perfect burn will usually be unattainable. In cases like this, select a wick that will burn well through the largest portion of the candle. For example, a wick that provides a good burn at the middle of a pyramid candle will be much too large at the top and a bit too small at the bottom. However, this will be the wick we need—sacrificing a good burn near the top for an acceptable burn in the bottom two-thirds of the candle.

Procedure

The actual procedure will vary with the type of mold as explained in chapter 10. The pouring temperature needed will vary as well, and it is usually best to follow the mold manufacturer's directions. If you do not have the mold instructions, start with 180 to 185° F (82 to 85° C). If this does not work out, gradually increase the pouring temperature on successive pours until the necessary pouring temperature is found.

17

Poured Candles— Intermediate Projects

Once you have mastered basic candle pouring, you are ready to move on to more advanced projects. This chapter contains many projects that are just a bit more difficult than plain poured candles. As with the beginner projects, try to master each technique before moving on to the next.

Cold-Pour Candles

Difficulty Rating: 4

Cold-poured candles require no additional effort, materials, or skills. Yet this technique adds much visual interest to finished candles. Cold-poured wax flows differently up the mold sides and also traps air bubbles. Years ago we used to remelt cold-pour candles as rejects, but lately their rustic appearance has become popular.

This technique may be used with most types of candles. Cold-pouring may be done successfully in votives, pillars, and clear containers. Although it may also be done on tea lights, opaque containers, and floating candles, the effect will not be visible since cold-pouring has no effect on the tops of top-up candles.

Cold pouring is a simple way to create unique candles.

Materials

The materials and equipment are the same as used for a plain candle. For example, to make a cold-poured pillar candle, use the same materials as a plain pillar candle.

Formula

Follow the recipe for the type of candle you are making as explained in chapter 16.

Procedure

The procedure will be the same as for a plain candle except for pouring temperature. A wide range of pouring temperatures may be used from about 150° F (66° C) down to about 115° F (46° C). The colder the pouring temperature, the more texture the finished candle will have.

For maximum texture, allow the wax to cool in the pouring pot until a surface film forms. Stir the film back into the wax, and then pour. When making cold-poured candles it is important to pour into the center of the mold—any wax splashed or dripped on the sides of the mold will be visible on the finished candle.

Variations

The instructions above are for a basic cold-pour candle. Other styles are possible as follows:

Layered

Any number of color layers may be used as explained for layered candles.

Ice

Use this technique in an ice-filled mold as explained for ice candles. Not to be used in containers.

Two-Tone Candles

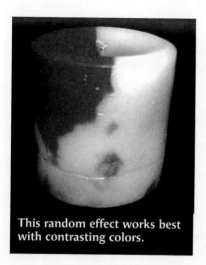

This random effect works best with contrasting colors.

Two-tone candles are a variation of cold-pouring. By allowing the wax to cool before pouring, we can pour two or more colors at the same time without them mixing together.

This technique works well with pillar molds and clear container candles. Other molds may be used, but it is much more difficult when using molds with a small top opening to pour the wax into.

Important: There is one rule that should always be followed when making two tone candles—the same wax formula should be used for each color. Failure to observe this rule may result in poor burning.

Materials

The materials and equipment are the same as you would use for a plain candle. For example, to make a two-tone pillar candle, use the same materials as a plain pillar candle. These instructions are for two-tone container candles. Additional materials needed:

• One pouring pot and heat source for each color to be used.

Formula

Follow the recipe for the type of candle you are making as explained in chapter 16.

Procedure

1. Prepare the wax formula for each color to be used and place on heat. They will be poured at the same time, so they must be prepared at the same time.

2. While the wax is melting, prepare your wick (prime and tab).

3. Affix the wick tab inside the container. This may be done with hot glue, tacky wax, or silicone caulk.

4. Once the wax is fully melted, add dye. Strongly contrasting colors work best. Note—red dyes tend to bleed more than other colors (just like clothing dye in the laundry).

5. Test the colors and add more dye as needed.

6. Add scent oil (optional). Stir well.

7. Remove the wax pots from heat and allow them to cool.

8. Check the wax periodically until a surface film begins to form.

9. Stir the surface film into the wax.

10. Pour both colors into the container at the same time.

11. Try to avoid splashing the sides of the container, as any splashes may be visible in the finished candle.

12. Set aside the leftover wax.

13. If a shrink void appears after cooling, reheat the wax and make a final pour ending flush with the top level of the first pour. Usually this is not necessary, as the cool wax does not shrink as much.

14. Once fully hardened, trim the wick to ¼ inch (6 mm).

Variations

The instructions above are for basic two-color candles. Other styles are possible as noted below:

Multicolored

Any number of colors may be used. If using three or more colors a helper will be needed since you will need more than two hands.

Ice

Use this technique in an ice-filled mold as explained for ice candles. Do not use in container candles.

Ice Candles

Difficulty Rating: 5

The size of the ice chunks has a big effect on the finished appearance.

Ice candles are also called lace candles because of the lacy open effect obtained from this technique. There are two main techniques used to make ice candles. One is very simple, but will not produce a high quality candle. With the simple technique, water may become trapped in the center of the candle, causing erratic burning. The better technique takes a bit more effort, but will provide a much higher quality finished candle.

This technique is best used with pillar candles. It will not work in containers because there is no way to get the water (from the melted ice) out.

Materials

In addition to the basic materials you will need:

- Mold—A pillar candle mold with a wide top.

- Ice—My preference is for crushed ice, but just about any size ice chunks may be used.

Ice Preparation

The appearance of the finished candle depends mostly on the size of the ice chunks used. Small pieces of ice will provide a lacier, more uniform look while larger pieces will give more of a freeform appearance. I find that pieces averaging about ⅜ inch (9 mm) work best. Optimally you will be able to obtain ice in the size desired, but usually you will have to break it up yourself.

1. Place the ice in a plastic bag.

2. Wrap the ice bag with a ¼ inch (6 mm) thick layer of newspaper or an old towel.

3. Place the wrapped bag on a hard surface.

4. Hit with a hammer until the ice is the desired size.

5. Place the bag of ice in a freezer until it is needed to prevent melting.

Simple Procedure

This procedure is the easiest way to make ice candles, and is the first candle many people ever make, since it is a popular project with scouts and other youth groups.

1. Prepare the wax formula and place on heat.

2. While the wax is melting, prepare your mold (mold release, wick, sealer).

As you can see, some of the ice is near the wick, which will cause air spaces that affect the burning.

3. Once the wax is fully melted, add dye.

4. Test the color and add more dye as needed.

5. Bring temperature to 185 to 190° F (85 to 88° C).

6. Add scent oil (optional). Stir well.

7. Pour a thin layer of wax into the mold. This should be ⅛ inch (3 mm) or less.

8. Remove the ice from the freezer, and fill the mold.

9. Immediately fill the mold with wax.

10. Set aside the leftover wax in case it is needed in step 12.

11. Allow the candle to cool.

12. If a shrink void or well appears after cooling, reheat the wax set aside in step 10 and make a final pour ending ¼ inch (6 mm) below the top level. This step is usually not required on ice candles.

13. Once the candle is fully hardened, hold the mold over a sink or bucket to catch the water. Remove the candle from the mold.

14. Trim the bottom wick.

15. Level the base.

16. Trim the top wick to ¼ inch (6 mm).

151

Improved Procedure

This procedure requires more effort, but produces a much higher quality candle. If you intend to sell your ice candles, this is the technique to use. By using a core candle, we prevent any water or air pockets from being trapped near the wick. Since more wax is in the center of the candle, it will also burn longer. You will use two molds for this project—one the size of the finished candle, and a smaller diameter mold for the core candle.

1. Prepare the wax formula and place on heat.

2. While the wax is melting, prepare your core candle mold (mold release, wick, sealer). This should be a round pillar of the same height as the finished candle, and 1½ to 2 inches (38 to 50 mm) in diameter.

3. Once the wax is fully melted, add dye.

4. Test the color and add more dye as needed.

5. Bring the temperature to 185 to 190° F (85 to 88° C).

6. Add scent oil (optional). Stir well.

7. Pour the core candle as a plain pillar candle. This is usually best done ahead of time, as it must be fully cooled before using in the ice candle.

8. Place the finished core candle into a larger mold by threading the wick through the wick hole and sealing with a putty-type mold sealer.

9. Pour a thin layer of wax into the mold. This should be ⅛ inch (3 mm) or less.

10. Remove the ice from the freezer, and fill the mold around the core candle with ice.

11. Immediately fill the mold with wax.

12. Set aside the leftover wax in case it is needed in step 14.

By using a core candle, we can prevent air spaces that affect the burning.

13. Allow the candle to cool.

14. If a shrink void or well appears after cooling, reheat the wax set aside in step 12 and make a final pour ending ¼ inch (6 mm) below the top level of the first pour. This step is rarely required with this ice candle technique.

15. Once fully hardened, hold mold over a sink or bucket to catch the water. Remove the candle from the mold.

16. Trim the bottom wick.

17. Level the base.

18. Trim the top wick to ¼ inch (6 mm).

Variations

The instructions above are for basic ice candles. Many other variants are possible as noted below:

Add Ice While Pouring

Adding the ice while pouring the wax gives a slightly different appearance that is preferred by some. This is much simpler to do with a helper, as it is difficult with only two hands.

Layers

Do not fill the mold all the way with ice. Pour just enough wax to cover the ice. Repeat for each additional layer.

Swiss Cheese

By coloring the wax a pale yellow and using a suitably shaped mold it is possible to make candles that look like Swiss cheese.

Burning

The holes and irregularities in ice candles make them more prone to dripping, so they should always be burned on a holder large enough to contain the dripping wax. On the simple style ice candles, the need to pour off trapped water or to trim the wick frequently is common.

Chunk Candles

Difficulty Rating: 5

Chunk candles have been very popular for a few decades. Chunk techniques provide a beautiful finished candle, yet are extremely simple to make. This technique may be used with most types of candles, but looks best in pillar or clear container candles.

Important: There is one rule that should always be followed when making chunk candles—always make the chunks with the same wax formula used for the fill wax. Failure to observe this rule may result in poor burning. Even worse is the possibility of a spout forming in

Chunk candles can be made in any mold and color combination.

the side and allowing the molten wax to pour out. This can be caused by a softer wax melting first (because of two different wax formulas).

Materials

These instructions are for chunk pillar candles. If making a different type, such as container chunk candles, substitute the materials and procedure for a candle of that type as explained in chapter 16. In addition to the basic materials you will need:

- Cake pans or cookie sheets.

- A pizza cutter or sharp utility knife.

- A wooden spoon.

Procedure

1. Prepare the wax formula for the first color and place on heat.

2. While the wax is melting, coat the pans with your choice of mold release.

3. Once the wax is fully melted, add dye.

4. Test the color and add more dye as needed.

5. Bring the temperature to 185 to 190° F (85 to 88° C).

6. Add scent oil (optional). Stir well.

7. Allow the wax to settle for 2 to 3 minutes. This will allow any residue, dirt, or dye particles to sink to the bottom of the pouring pot.

8. Pour the wax into the pans. If small chunks are desired, pour a thin layer—⅛ to 3/16 inch (3 to 5 mm) thick. For larger chunks a thicker layer should be poured. The thickness should be kept to ⅜ inch (9 mm) for ease of cutting. If irregular chunk sizes are desired, elevate one end of the pan slightly.

9. Allow the wax to cool until it is firm to the touch. The edges will cool first, and you will see a noticeable difference as the wax cools.

10. While the wax is still warm, use the knife or pizza cutter to cut the chunks. Chunks may be cut in uniform or irregular sizes.

A pizza cutter makes quick work of cutting chunks.

11. Allow the chunks to cool fully.

12. Once cooled, the chunks should be easy to remove from the pan. Place them in a bag or other clean container.

13. Repeat the above steps for each color needed.

14. Once you have accumulated enough chunks in the desired colors, prepare the fill wax and place on heat. This should be the same formula as the chunks, however it looks best when no dye is added to the fill wax.

15. Prepare your mold (mold release, wick, sealer). Beginners should use molds 3 inches (75 mm) or less in diameter.

16. Fill the mold with chunks. This may be done randomly, or in a pattern such as layers of colored chunks.

17. Because the chunks will have a cooling effect on the hot wax, it will be necessary to pour at a hotter temperature than normal to prevent a cold-pour effect. The larger the mold, the hotter the wax will need to be. Bring the wax to 195 to 200° F (91 to 93° C). To obtain a hotter temperature for larger molds, it is necessary to go to direct heat, which is discussed in chapter 18 for the blended chunks project.

18. Pour the wax into the center of the candle (next to the wick). This will prevent the hot wax from melting the chunks unevenly on the outside of the mold where it would be visible on the finished candle. Set aside the leftover wax for step 21.

19. Using the flat part of the wooden spoon, gently tap the mold sides to shake loose any air bubbles trapped by the chunks.

20. Allow the candle to cool. While cooling, poke two or three relief holes near the wick. This will help the second pour adhere.

21. Once the candle is fully hardened, reheat the wax set aside in step 18.

22. Pour into the mold to fill the shrink hole. Stop the pour ¼ inch (6 mm) below the level of the first pour.

23. When the second pour has cooled, remove the candle from the mold.

24. Trim the bottom wick, then level the base.

25. Trim the top wick to ¼ inch (6 mm).

Variations

The instructions above are for basic chunk candles. Many other styles are possible as noted below:

Colored Fill

The fill wax may be colored. Light colors work best.

Irregular Chunks

For irregular chunks, allow the sheets to harden, then remove them from the pans and break the chunks off instead of cutting them.

Patterned Chunks

Make the chunks in small molds (such as floating candle molds, or patterned ice cube trays) to create chunks with a distinct shape.

Layers

Alternate fill wax colors.

Cold-Pour

Use cold-pour techniques on the fill wax.

Multicolored

Any number of colors may be used.

Monochrome Color

Use only different shades of the one color.

Blended Chunks

See the blended chunks project in chapter 18.

Torching

Use a torch or heat gun on the surface of the candle. Same as for the torched candle project explained in chapter 18.

Beer Candles

Difficulty Rating: 5

This project is rather special in that it is a container candle with a surface technique applied to it. It is relatively simple to do, yet looks difficult. These candles make great gifts for beer lovers, and can be scented if desired (though I have yet to find a scent oil that really smells like beer).

This technique may be applied to simulate any carbonated beverage.

Materials

This type of candle can be considered a container candle. In addition to the basic materials you will need:

- Beer mug—Or a glass, if you prefer.

- Low melt point paraffin wax—I like to use a melt point of 130° F (55° C).

- Opaquing hardener—Such as Vybar or Stearic.

• Dyes—Yellow suits most folks, but for darker beer add a bit of harvest gold or brown to the yellow.

• Cored wick and tab—Of a size suitable for the diameter of your container.

• Blender or whisk—For whipping wax.

• Fork—A regular dinner fork.

Procedure

1. Place the wax on heat. Do not mix in any additives, since we want a translucent effect in the candle.

2. Prime and tab a wick about 2 inches (5 cm) longer than the container.

3. Attach the wick to a wick bar so that the tab suspends slightly above the bottom of the container. This will make it less visible in the finished candle.

4. Set the wick aside for later.

5. Bring the wax to 185° F (85° C).

6. Add dye until the wax is your desired color.

7. Add scent if desired.

8. Allow the wax to settle for 2 to 3 minutes.

9. Pour the wax into the container, stopping about ¾ inch (19 mm) from the top. Set aside the leftover wax for step 12.

10. Insert the wick, centering it as well as possible.

11. Allow the candle to cool for 30 minutes, then poke 2 or 3 relief holes near the wick.

12. After one hour, reheat the wax from step 9.

13. Repour the shrink void, stopping the pour ¼ inch (6 mm) below the level of the first pour.

14. Allow the candle to cool completely.

15. Remove the wick bar and straighten the wick.

16. Add some opaquing hardener to the remaining wax and place it back on heat.

17. Remove the wax from the heat source as soon as it liquefies.

18. As the wax cools, periodically whip it with a whisk or hand blender.

19. Repeat step 18 until the wax is the consistency of runny cooked oatmeal.

20. Use the fork to pick up blobs of the whipped wax and drop them on the top of the candle. Continue until it resembles a nice foamy head. Letting some overflow the top to run partway down the side looks very realistic, but makes the candle more fragile.

21. Once the candle cools, trim the wick to ¼ inch (6 mm).

Variations

The beer candle concept can be applied to any similar beverage. Here are a few suggestions:

Soda Pop

Use different colors to represent your beverage of choice.

Cappuccino

Make in a coffee cup.

Straws

Adding a straw or two increases the illusion, especially for soda pop candles. But it also makes them more dangerous to burn (straws may catch fire). If you opt for adding straws, try to keep them as far from the wick as possible.

Faux Straws

Cut the straws to 2 inches (5 cm) and push into the very edge of the whipped wax. This is much safer, but still not 100 percent safe.

Fireplace Candles

Difficulty Rating: 5

Fireplace candles are sometimes referred to as mantel candles. Essentially, they are long narrow candles with multiple wicks. In the late 1990's, these became very popular and a wide variety of sizes and shapes became available. Some companies went so far as to offer special holders to accommodate their shape.

Although some mold manufacturers now offer rectangular molds of

This candle style will let you use your fireplace in warm weather.

this type, these instructions will explain how to make one with a standard pillar candle mold. Should you choose to purchase a specialty mold for these, the procedure is the same as the basic pillar candle.

Materials

This project uses the basic pillar candle materials and recipe. In addition to the basic materials you will need:

- Mold—A round or square pillar mold of 3 inches (7.5 cm) diameter or less works well. A height of 9 to 12 inches (22.5 to 30 cm) is suitable.

- Drill—A drill press works best, but if you don't have access to one, a hand drill may be used.

- Drill bit—A drill bit slightly larger than your wick diameter and long enough to pass through the candle's diameter will be needed.

Procedure

1. Prepare the wax formula and place it on your heat source.

2. Coat the mold with mold release.

3. Seal the wick hole with putty or a plug—no wick is used at this point.

4. Once the wax is fully melted, add dye.

5. Test the color and add more dye as needed.

6. Bring the temperature to 185 to 190° F (85 to 88° C).

7. Add scent oil (optional). Stir well.

8. Allow the wax to settle for 2 to 3 minutes. This will allow any residue, dirt, or undissolved dye particles to sink to the bottom of the pouring pot.

9. Pour the wax into the mold.

10. Set aside the leftover wax for step 13.

11. Allow the candle to cool fully.

12. While the candle is cooling, poke two or three relief holes in the center. This will help the second pour adhere better.

13. Once the candle is fully hardened, reheat the wax set aside in step 10.

14. Pour into the mold to fill the shrink hole. Stop the pour ¼ inch (6 mm) below the level of the first pour.

15. When the second pour has cooled, remove the candle from the mold.

16. Level the base.

17. Holding the candle horizontally, level a flat spot along the length (on round candles only). This will prevent the finished candle from rolling.

18. Use the drill press or hand drill to make evenly spaced wick holes along the top of the candle in a straight line down the center.

19. Insert wicks. This is much easier if the wicks have been primed.

Variations

The instructions above are for plain fireplace candles. Many other styles are possible as noted below:

Cold Pour

Use cold-pour techniques.

Chunks

These may be made using chunk candle techniques.

Blended Chunks

See the blended chunks project in chapter 18.

Torching

Use a torch or heat gun on the surface of the candle. This technique is explained in chapter 18.

Whipped Wax

Whipped wax may be applied to the finished candle for a frosted look. Explained in chapter 16.

Layered Candles

Difficulty Rating: 6

This is an early decorative technique that is still popular today.

Layered candles have also been around for a long time. Layering techniques require a bit of practice to master, yet are still fairly simple. This technique may be used with most types of candles, but it looks best in pillar or clear container candles.

In their simplest form, layered candles are simply two different colors of wax poured into the mold at different times. Of course the possibilities don't end there. Many layers, many colors, angled layers, even combining layering with other techniques—all are possible. Some exceptionally talented folks can even create landscapes with layering by manipulating the previously poured wax layers with spoons and sticks to create rivers, mountains and trees.

Important: There is one rule that should always be followed when making layered candles—every layer should be made from the same wax formula. Failure to observe this rule may result in poor burning.

Timing

In theory, layered candles are extremely simple. In practice, the technique is simple, but the timing between pours takes quite a bit of practice. Before proceeding, it is important to understand the factors affecting the timing of each pour.

• Mass of wax—The larger the body of hot wax, the longer it will take to cool. Factors affecting mass are layer thickness and mold diameter.

• Pouring temperature—This is pretty obvious. The hotter you pour, the longer the wax takes to cool.

• Mold material—Some mold materials retain heat more than others.

• Room temperature—Although it is not a major factor most of the time, be aware that the cooling time needed will be shorter in colder room temperatures and longer in higher room temperatures.

The above information should make it very obvious that timing pours with a watch is impractical because of all the factors that affect cooling time. Even something as simple as different thickness layers will affect the cooling time. With time and practice you will develop a feel for the proper timing.

Materials

These instructions are for layered pillar candles. If you are making a different type, such as layered container candles, substitute the materials and procedure for a candle of that type as explained in chapter 16. In addition to the basic materials you will need:

• One pouring pot and heat source for each color to be used.

Procedure

1. Prepare the wax formula for each color to be used and place on heat. For most candles of this type you will not have enough time between each pouring to melt the next color, so they must be prepared at the same time.

2. While the wax is melting, prepare your mold (mold release, wick, sealer).

3. Once the first batch of wax is fully melted, add dye. Strongly contrasting colors work best. *Note*—Red dyes tend to bleed more than other colors (just like clothing dye in the laundry).

4. Test your first color and add more dye as needed.

5. Bring the temperature to 185 to 190° F (85 to 88° C).

6. Add scent oil (optional). Stir well.

7. Allow the wax to settle for 2 to 3 minutes. This will allow any residue, dirt, or undissolved dye particles to sink to the bottom of the pouring pot.

8. Pour the first layer of wax into the mold. Try to avoid splashing the sides of the mold, as any splashes may be visible in the finished candle.

9. While the first pour is cooling, prepare the second pour (dye, temperature, and so on) for immediate use when needed as explained below.

10. Allow the layer to cool until the wax is firm to the touch, but before the wax cools enough to separate from the mold. This is the critical step. If you pour too soon, the two colors will blend. If you pour too late, after the first pour has separated from the mold, the second pour will run between the first pour and the mold, which will be unsightly and make mold removal difficult.

11. Pour the next color, again taking care to avoid splashing the mold sides.

12. Repeat steps 10 and 11 for each additional layer desired.

13. If a shrink void appears in the final layer after cooling, reheat the same color and make a final pour ending ¼ inch (6 mm) below the top level.

14. Once the entire candle is fully hardened, remove it from the mold.

15. Trim the bottom wick.

16. Level the base.

17. Trim the top wick to ¼ inch (6 mm).

Variations

The instructions above are for basic horizontally layered pillar candles. Many other styles are possible as noted below:

Angled Layers

Tilt the mold by placing a pencil or something of similar thickness under one side of the mold.

Variable Angled Layers

Before each pour change the angle of the mold.

Mixed Angled and Horizontal Layers

Any combination of horizontal and tilted layers.

Multicolored

Any number of colors may be used.

Monochrome Color

Each layer is poured in a different shade of the same color.

Progressive Color

This variant of monochrome color starts with a light color. For each successive pour, a bit more dye of the same color is added.

Thin Stripe

A two-color candle that is mostly one color with a thin ¼ to ⅜ inch (6 to 9 mm) layer of a highly contrasting color in the middle gives a striking effect.

Blended Stripes

By reducing the time between each pour, it is possible to get each layer to blend slightly with the previous one providing a subtle transition. This is especially effective with the progressive color variation. Timing is everything with this technique. If you pour too soon, the entire layer will blend fully and not produce the subtle blend desired between layers. If you pour too late, the layers will not blend. If you pour really late, the wax will run between the mold and the previous layer, ruining the candle.

Combinations

Any mixture of the above techniques may be combined for an even wider variety of possible variations.

Mottled Candles

Difficulty Rating: 6

Mottling appears as snowflakes in the wax.

Mottled candles have seen a huge surge in popularity in recent years. Although years ago we usually considered these defective, they have a distinct look with "character" that makes them popular in today's market. The mottling is caused by a chemical reaction in the wax caused by too much oil. The effect ranges from tiny "snowflakes" to a grainy appearance within the wax.

Paraffin is a petroleum product, and as such it has oil content. Mottling is achieved by adding additional oil. Mottling takes place in a narrow range of total oil content. Too little and no mottling occurs, too much and the oil weeps out of the wax. Cooling time also affects mottling. Generally it is much easier to mottle large candles, since they cool slower than small candles. When attempting to mottle small candles, it is often necessary to slow the cooling by placing a box over the mold to retain the heat.

Important—Many polymer-type additives, such as Vybar, will inhibit mottling and should never be used when attempting mottled candles.

Materials

The materials and equipment are the same as used for a plain candle of that type as explained in chapter 16, with the following exceptions:

- Paraffin Wax—Use a pure, non-blended paraffin wax. I recommend 140° F (60° C) melt point for molded candles and 130° F (54° C) melt point for container and votive candles.

- Stearic Acid—Stearic will harden the wax without inhibiting mottling when used in moderation.

- Mottling agent—The most easily obtained mottling agents are scent oil, carrier oil (unscented oil), or mineral oil (a laxative available in your local pharmacy). Some solid mottling agents are available commercially, but are more difficult to find. I have had mixed results with solid mottling agents, so I prefer to use oil.

Formulas

Molded Candles

1 pound (454 grams) 140° F (60° C) melt point paraffin
3 tablespoons of stearic acid—Approximately 1 ounce
Mottling Agent—The exact quantity needed will vary from wax to wax since different waxes have different oil content. A good starting point for experimentation is a total of 2 tablespoons of oil. This may be all one type of oil or a combination of oils. For example, 1 tablespoon scent oil and 1 tablespoon of mineral oil. If you are using a dry mottling agent, follow the manufacturer's instructions.
Dye as desired

Container/Votive Candles

1 pound 130° F (54° C) melt point paraffin
3 tablespoons stearic acid—Approximately 1 ounce.
Mottling Agent—The exact quantity needed will vary from wax to wax
since different waxes have different oil content. A good starting point
for experimentation is a total of 2 tablespoons of oil. This may be all
one type of oil or a combination of oils. If you are using a dry mottling
agent, follow the manufacturer's instructions.
Dye as desired

Procedure

This procedure is for molded candles. For other types of candles, refer to the appropriate instructions in chapter 16.

1. Prepare the wax formula and place on heat.

2. While the wax is melting, prepare your mold or container.

3. Once the wax is fully melted, add dye. Test colors and add more dye as needed.

4. Bring the temperature to 190 to 195° F (88 to 91° C).

5. Add the mottling agent. Stir well.

6. Pour the wax into the mold.

7. Set aside the leftover wax for use in step 10.

8. It is necessary for the candle to cool slowly in order to allow time for the reaction that causes mottling. Very large molds will often mottle with no additional effort. Smaller molds will usually benefit from placing a box over them to retain some of the heat and slow the cooling process.

THE DEGREE OF MOTTLING
WILL VARY WITH DIFFERENT
COOLING SPEEDS.

9. Allow the candle to cool.

10. Reheat the leftover wax from step 7.

11. Pour into the mold to fill the shrink void. Stop pour at ¼ inch (6 mm) below the level of the first pour.

12. Once the candle is fully hardened, remove it from the mold.

13. Trim the bottom wick.

14. Level the base.

15. Trim the top wick to ¼ inch (6 mm).

Troubleshooting

The instructions above are general guidelines for mottled candle experimentation. After each experimental candle is made, use the information below to adjust the formula for additional experiments until you have a formula that works well with your wax.

SYMPTOM	CAUSE	CURE
Oil seepage or candle that feels excessively oily	Too much oil has been added, and oil content is beyond the capacity of the wax to hold it.	Reduce total oil added
Very little mottling	Mostly seen in small candles. Usually caused by the wax cooling before full mottling occurs.	Slow the cooling process. Pouring at a higher temperature will sometimes help this.

Symptom	Cause	Cure
Not mottling at all	Usually caused by insufficient mottling agents, but sometimes caused by cooling too fast. Some additives such as Vybar inhibit mottling.	Increase the amount of mottling agent. If the wax cannot hold more oil, then the problem is most likely related to cooling speed. Do not use Vybar.

Vertical Stripe Candles

Difficulty Rating: 6

This variation of chunk candles can be used to create vertically striped candles. The process is very simple. This technique requires the use of a straight-sided mold.

Important—There is one rule that should always be followed when making chunk type candles—always make the chunks with the same wax formula used for the fill wax. Failure to observe this rule may result in poor burning or a spout forming in the side, allowing the molten wax to pour out.

Materials

In addition to the basic materials you will need:

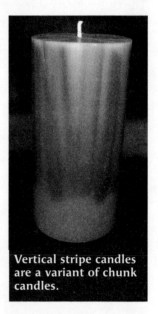

Vertical stripe candles are a variant of chunk candles.

• Straight sided mold

• Cake pans or cookie sheets

• A pizza cutter or sharp utility knife

• A wooden spoon

Procedure

1. Prepare the wax formula for the first color and place on heat.

2. While the wax is melting, coat the pans with mold release.

3. Once the wax is fully melted, add dye.

4. Test the color and add more dye as needed.

5. Bring the temperature to 185 to 190° F (85 to 88° C).

6. Add scent oil (optional). Stir well.

7. Allow the wax to settle for 2 to 3 minutes. This will allow any residue, dirt, or undissolved dye particles to sink to the bottom of the pouring pot.

8. Pour the wax into the pans. The thickness should be kept to about ⅜ inch (9 mm) for ease of cutting.

9. Allow the wax to cool until it is firm to the touch. The edges will cool first, and you will see a noticeable difference as the wax cools.

10. While the wax is still warm, use the knife or pizza cutter to cut the wax into long strips. Strips may be cut in uniform or irregular sizes. The strips will need to be as long as the mold is tall.

11. Allow the cut strips to cool fully.

12. Once cooled, the strips should be easy to remove from the pan. Place them in a bag or other clean container.

13. Repeat the above steps for each color desired.

14. Once you have accumulated enough strips in the desired colors to fill the mold, prepare the fill wax and place on heat. This should be the same formula as the chunks; however, it looks best when no dye is added to the fill wax.

15. Prepare your mold (mold release, wick, sealer). Beginners should use molds 3 inches (75 mm) or less in diameter.

16. Lay the mold on its side. This will allow you to position the strips more easily.

17. Fill the mold with strips. This may be done randomly, or in a pattern such as alternating colors. If you are creating a pattern, fill the mold from side to side before beginning the next row.

18. Because the strips will have a cooling effect on the hot wax, it is necessary to pour at a hotter temperature than normal to prevent a cold-pour effect. The larger the mold, the hotter the wax will need to be. Bring the wax to 195 to 200° F (91 to 93° C). To obtain a hotter temperature for larger molds, it is necessary to go to direct heat, which is discussed in chapter 18 for the Blended Chunks Project.

19. Pour the wax into the center of the candle (next to the wick). This will prevent the hot wax from melting the strips unevenly on the outside of the mold, where it would be visible on the finished candle.

20. Set aside the leftover wax for step 23.

21. Using the flat part of the wooden spoon, gently tap the mold sides to shake loose any air bubbles trapped by the chunks.

22. Allow the candle to cool. While the candle is cooling, poke two or three relief holes near the wick. This will help the second pour adhere.

23. Once the candle is fully hardened, reheat the wax set aside in step 20.

24. Pour the reheated wax into the mold to fill the shrink hole. Stop the pour ¼ inch (6 mm) below the level of the first pour.

25. When the second pour has cooled, remove the candle from the mold.

26. Trim the bottom wick.

27. Level the base.

28. Trim the top wick to ¼ inch (6 mm).

Variations

The instructions above are for basic vertical stripe pillar candles. Many other styles are possible as noted below:

Colored Fill

The fill wax may be colored. Light colors work best.

Layers

Alternate fill wax colors.

Cold Pour

Use cold-pour techniques on the fill wax.

Multicolored

Any number of colors may be used.

Monochrome Color

Use only different shades of the one color.

Blended Vertical Stripes

Use very high pouring temperature. Use the procedure for the blended chunks project in chapter 18.

Torching

Use a torch or heat gun on the surface of the candle. Explained in chapter 18.

Water Candles

Difficulty Rating: 6

Because of its ability to rapidly cool wax, water can be used to create some of the most unique candles possible. This technique is very simple, and well within the capabilities of any candle maker. The core candle must be made with the appropriate wax formula for that candle type. The fill wax should be a floating candle or pillar formula.

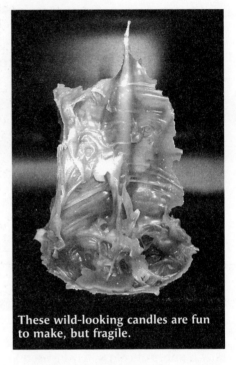

These wild-looking candles are fun to make, but fragile.

Materials

In addition to the basic materials you will need:

- Core candle—This should be a small pillar or taper candle about 6 inches (15 cm) long. This may be made or bought.

- Pie pan—I recommend a 6-inch (15-cm) diameter to start with. Disposable pans are easiest to set up, but if you decide to make a lot of these candles you will probably want to a more substantial one.

- Wire—A yard or meter of wire will be needed for handles. The exact type and gauge of the wire is not critical as long as it is sturdy enough to use for handles and flexible enough to bend easily.

- Nail—To punch holes in the pan.

- Hammer—To hit the nail.

• Wire cutter—To cut the wire to length.

• Water bucket—This must be several inches taller and wider than the candles you plan to make.

Preparation

A water candle jig needs to be made before starting. This will allow you to easily handle the pan of hot wax without burning yourself.

1. Place the pan upside down on a hard surface such as a scrap of wood.

2. Mark the hole placement on the rim of the pan. First mark one pair of holes 1¼ inches (3.1 cm) apart. Mark a second pair of holes on the opposite side of the pan.

This easy-to-make jig will allow you to make water candles with ease.

3. Use the hammer and nail to punch a hole at each mark.

4. Cut two pieces of wire 18 to 20 inches (45 to 50 cm) long.

5. Bend a piece of wire and insert through one pair of holes from the top.

6. Twist the ends together to keep the wire from pulling out of the holes.

7. Repeat steps 5 and 6 for the second pair of holes.

8. The jig is now ready to use.

Formula

Since the wax used will be external to the core candle, the exact formula used is not critical. This is a good project to use up your scrap wax on. If you have no scraps and need to mix the wax, use whatever floating candle formula you prefer.

Procedure

1. Prepare the wax formula and place on heat.

2. Fill the water bucket. Do not fill it to the top, to allow for displacement.

3. Once the wax is fully melted, add dye.

4. Test the color and add more dye as needed.

5. Bring the temperature to 185 to 190° F (85 to 88° C).

6. Pour a ¼ inch (6 mm) layer of wax in the bottom of the pie pan.

7. Place the core candle into the wax, in the center of the pan.

8. Allow the wax layer to cool. This will secure the core candle into the pan.

9. Fill the pan with wax.

10. Lift your jig by the handles and dip it into the water bucket.

11. If the candle is satisfactory, it is complete.

12. Steps 9 and 10 may be repeated if desired.

Variations

The water candle effect is totally random and we have very little control over the final appearance. The techniques below may be used to vary the appearance:

Dipping Speed

The wax shapes formed will vary with the speed that the pan is dipped in the water.

Rotating

Rotate the pan as it enters the water.

Multicolored

Repeat steps 9 and 10 with a different color each time.

Mushroom Candles

Difficulty Rating: 6

An adaptation of sand-off sand casting, this technique uses sand to mold the wax in place of a more traditional mold. In this example we will be combining two separately molded shapes to create a mushroom-shaped candle, but the technique may be applied to any shape desired. The mold cavities can be formed with found objects, but feel free to shape the cavities by hand if you prefer.

This technique makes beautiful candles without store-bought molds.

The basic concept is that wet sand will retain the shape desired and hold the hot wax. Because we desire a fairly smooth surface, we will use relatively wet sand. This helps keep the wax from seeping between the grains.

Materials

This type of candle can be considered a basic pillar (molded) candle. In addition to the basic materials you will need:

• Sand—Medium grit sand works well, but the exact type is not critical.

• Bucket or tray—To hold the sand.

• Water

• Rounded bowl—4 to 6 inches (10 to 15 cm) in diameter. This will be used to form the mushroom cap.

• Metal votive mold or bottle—For forming the stem of the mushroom. If a taller stem is preferred, use a suitably shaped bottle.

• Two metal rods—To form wick holes. Thick wire or pieces of coat hanger may be used. These must be very straight, with no bumps, bends, or ridges.

• Heat gun or propane torch—Used to melt the two parts together. If you do not have access to either, tacky wax may be used to adhere the parts.

Procedure

1. Prepare the wax formula and place on heat.

2. Put sand in your bucket or tray to a depth 2 to 3 inches (5 to 8 cm) deeper than the object you plan to mold.

3. Wet the sand thoroughly.

4. Level the surface of the sand.

5. Press the bowl into the sand to form the mushroom cap mold. Remove the bowl.

6. If the cavity does not retain its shape, the sand is not wet enough. Return to step 3.

7. Form a separate mold cavity for the stem by pressing the votive or bottle into the sand narrow end down. Remove the mold from the sand.

The prepared sand ready to pour.

8. Insert the rods or wires through the center of the mold cavities into the sand. Make sure they are vertical for best results. The holes formed by these rods will simplify wicking the candle later. If you prefer to drill the holes instead, omit this step.

9. Now that the mold is prepared, add color and/or scent to the wax, and bring it to a pouring temperature of 160° F (71° C). Avoid pouring at hotter temperatures, as this will cause sand to stick to the wax.

10. Pour the wax slowly into the two mold cavities. Some folks like to hold a spoon inside the cavity upside down, and pour onto the spoon. This will help prevent the wax from gouging a hole in the sand (thus distorting the shape).

11. Set aside leftover wax for step 13.

12. Allow the poured wax to cool.

13. If necessary, make a second pour using the wax from step 11.

14. Allow the molded wax to cool completely.

15. Remove the two parts from the sand. Brush off any sand that has stuck to the wax.

16. Remove the rods from step 8 to open the wick holes. If you chose to drill instead, drill a hole through the center of both parts now.

17. Level the top and bottom of the stem as you would level the base of a candle.

18. Thread a wick through the two parts. When choosing a wick, calculate it for the diameter of the stem, not the cap.

19. With the wick threaded, lay the cap upside down. Hold the stem in one hand a short distance up the wick.

20. Use the heat gun or torch to liquefy the area around the wick on the cap.

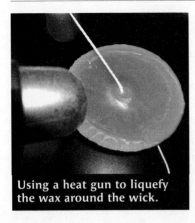

Using a heat gun to liquefy the wax around the wick.

21. Immediately slide the stem into place and allow the wax to cool.

22. Trim the wick flush with stem bottom.

23. Trim the top wick end to ¼ inch (6 mm).

Variations

The appearance of the basic mushroom candle can be enhanced with a variety of techniques. Here are a few suggestions:

Other Shapes

Obviously mushrooms aren't the only shapes possible with this technique, and with a bit of thought you will find many interesting shapes to use with this technique.

Chunk

Fill the mold cavities with colored wax chunks.

Two Color

Use a different color for each part.

Layered

Use the layered candle technique.

Ice

Use the ice candle technique.

Whipped Wax

Apply this surface technique to the cap to create texture.

Dripping

Drip wax of a contrasting color over the cap. This should be dyed to a very deep color or colored with pigments. For better adhesion, use a sculpting wax formula for this.

18

Poured Candles— Advanced Projects

$\mathcal{N}$ow that you have mastered a variety of moderately difficult candle styles, it is time to try some more challenging projects. This chapter contains projects that are about as difficult as candles can be. Rest assured, this does not mean you need a Ph.D. in candle making, just that it may take a few practice tries to get it right. As with the beginner projects, try to master each technique before moving on to the next.

Blended Chunk Candles

Difficulty Rating: 7

Although only slightly more difficult than regular chunk candles, this project does require direct heat. This style actually melts the chunks and fill wax together to get a smooth transition as opposed to sharply delineated chunks.

Materials

The materials and equipment are the same as used for a regular chunk candle.

Procedure

The procedure will be the same as for a regular chunk candle except for the pouring temperature. A wide range of pouring temperatures may be used from about 250° F (121° C) to about 325° F (163° C). The larger the mold, the hotter the pouring temperature I use.

Using hotter fill wax will cause your chunks to melt into the fill.

Warning: These pouring temperatures require heating the wax on direct heat. A thermometer is mandatory. Never heat wax above 325° F (163° C). Do not leave it unattended at all as the temperature will rise very fast. While the wax is on direct heat, do not be distracted by anything. If you need to answer the phone or door, remove the wax from the heat. A review of chapter 2 would be a wise idea before attempting this type of candle.

Snow Molded Candles

Difficulty Rating: 7

Snow molding is a fun technique that uses snow as the actual mold. The process produces a unique candle, and no two are alike. The major disadvantage of this technique is that it requires a lot of snow.

Materials

In addition to the materials and equipment used for a basic pillar candle, a bucket to hold the snow will be needed. This can also be done directly in a tightly packed snow bank, but the bucket technique is easier.

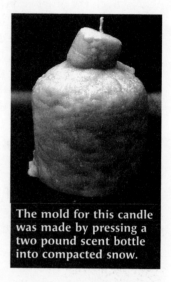

The mold for this candle was made by pressing a two pound scent bottle into compacted snow.

Formula

Any molded candle/pillar candle formula will work.

Procedure

1. Prepare the wax as for any molded candle.

2. While the wax is melting, collect a bucket of snow.

3. Use your hands or an object to create the shape desired for the candle in the snow. Make sure the snow is packed tightly.

4. Leave the bucket outdoors until the wax is ready for use.

5. Prime a length of wicking.

6. Push one end of the wick about 2 inches (5 cm) into the snow at bottom of the shaped cavity. If the wick is not stiff enough to make its own hole, a pilot hole may be made with a piece of wire, skewer, knitting needle, etc.

7. Attach the other end of the wick to a wick bar, dowel, or pencil.

8. Hold a spoon upside down inside the cavity. Pour the wax onto the spoon at 160° F (71° C). The spoon will help scatter the wax, preventing it from distorting the cavity shape.

9. Set aside the leftover wax and allow the candle to cool.

10. Once the wax is cool, reheat the leftover wax and repour the shrink void if necessary.

11. Once the candle is fully cooled, remove it from the from snow.

12. Finish as you would any molded candle—level the base and trim the wick.

Torched Candles

The variety possible with torching is unlimited.

Difficulty Rating: 8

Torching is an amazingly fun way to create some truly unique candles. Although the technique may be applied to almost any candle, for this project I have chosen to over-dip a star pillar candle in a variety of colors.

Materials

In addition to the materials and equipment as used for a basic candle, the following items will be needed:

- Dipping vats—One per color.

- Water bucket—For use between color dips.

- Pigments—Contrasting colors work best.

- Paraffin wax—Medium melt point paraffin works well.

- Hardener—Optional. I usually do not add a hardener to my dipping wax.

- Torch—A small propane or butane torch allows the most control. A heat gun may also be used.

- Large pan—When torching, lots of wax will melt off.

- Heat resistant surface—It is a good idea to place the pan on a surface that will not be a problem if exposed to excessive heat.

- Aluminum foil—To protect the wick when torching.

Formula

Any molded candle or pillar candle formula will work for the core candle.

Procedure

1. Make or purchase core candles. If you make them, leave the wicks long for ease of dipping.

2. Fill your vats with wax and place on a heat source. Try to regulate the temperature to about 155° F (68° C).

3. Add pigments to the wax. Follow supplier's instructions for pigment. If no instructions were supplied, start with ½ ounce (14 grams) per pound (454 grams). Add more if the desired coverage is not obtained.

4. Dip the candle in the first color. The very first dip only should be held in the wax for 30 seconds.

Starting at the top will minimize drip marks.

5. Dip the candle in water.

6. Repeat steps 4 and 5 until the desired depth of color is reached.

7. Repeat steps 4 through 6 with each additional color.

8. Once the candle has the desired layers of color, the real fun begins.

9. Place the pan on your heat resistant surface and set the candle in the pan.

10. Wrap a small piece of aluminum foil around the wick to protect it from the torch.

11. Fire up the torch.

12. Starting near the top of the candle, play the flame across the candle surface. Keep it moving.

13. Melt any pattern you like, but be sure to work from the top down.

14. Finish as you would any molded candle—level and trim the wick.

Balloon Candles

Difficulty Rating: 8

This is another old technique that is seeing some recent popularity. The concept is simple—a water-filled balloon is dipped into hot wax repeatedly until a shell forms. The shell is then further decorated if desired. The shell may be used as a candleholder or filled with wax to form a candle.

A filled balloon candle.

Materials

In addition to the materials and equipment used for a basic molded candle, the following will be needed:

- Dipping vat—To dip the balloon in.

- Water bucket—For use between color dips.

- Balloons—The balloon will undergo a lot of stress, so it is important to purchase thick, quality balloons.

- Goggles—There is always the possibility that the balloon will pop and splatter hot wax, so you need to protect your eyes.

Formula

Any molded candle or pillar candle formula will work for this technique. It is a good idea to add extra hardener (50 to 100 percent more) if you plan to use them as candleholders. If a translucent shell is desired, substitute a non-opaquing hardener.

Procedure

1. Fill the vat with wax and place it on a heat source. Try to regulate the temperature to about 155° F (68° C).

2. Add color to the wax if desired.

3. Fill the balloon with cold water to the approximate diameter you wish the finished candle to be. The water is vital, so do not omit this step. Air-filled balloons tend to break.

4. Dip the balloon in the wax.

5. Dip in water.

6. Repeat steps 4 and 5 until the desired thickness is reached. For most applications a ¼ inch (6 mm) shell is good.

7. Once the wax is fully hardened, pop the balloon while holding it over a sink. Remove the balloon.

8. Level the base so it will sit without rolling around.

9. Level the top to provide a smooth clean edge.

10. If you plan on using the shell as is, you are done.

11. Prepare a primed and tabbed wick, and place it in the shell.

12. Melt some wax. Use any standard molded or pillar candle formula.

13. As soon as the wax is melted, add color and scent. Remove the wax from the heat. The object here is to pour it at the lowest possible temperature to prevent damage to the wax shell.

14. Add the wax to the shell one spoonful at a time, allowing it to cool between each spoonful.

Add cool wax to the balloon shell one spoon at a time to prevent heat distortion.

15. Once the shell is filled, trim the wick to ¼ inch (6 mm).

Variations

The basic balloon candle may be enhanced in a variety of ways:

Color Fill

Make a translucent shell, and then fill with colored wax.

Colored Drips

Make a translucent shell, and then drip colored wax on the inside.

Cutouts

Use a drill or heated knife to cut windows in the shell. Cover the windows with masking tape, and fill the shell with a contrasting wax.

Sea Shore Candles

Difficulty Rating: 8

This technique is similar to the mushroom candle project. The main difference is that for this project we want the sand to stick to the wax. Also called sand-on sand casting, this technique uses the sand as both a mold and a decorative element. The technique may be applied to any shape desired.

The wet sand will retain the shape desired, hold the embedded objects in place, and hold the hot wax. Because we desire the sand to adhere to the wax, we will use relatively dry sand. This helps the wax seep between the grains.

Materials

This type of candle can be considered a basic pillar (molded) candle. In addition to the basic materials you will need:

• Sand—Medium grit sand works well, but the exact type is not critical.

• Bucket or tray—To hold the sand.

• Water

• Sea Shells

• Driftwood—Small pieces work best, optional.

• Primed and tabbed wicks—Suitably sized for your candle.

Seashells and driftwood are a natural addition to sand candles.

• Heat gun or propane torch—Used to put a nice finish on the sand portion, optional.

• Protective clothing—Goggles, long sleeve shirt, and gloves are recommended for step 9.

Procedure

1. Prepare the wax formula and place on heat. Do not add any scent or color for the initial pour.

2. Put sand in your bucket or tray to a depth 2 to 3 inches (5 to 8 cm) deeper than the object you plan to mold.

3. Wet the sand thoroughly. Use just enough water to allow the sand to hold its shape.

4. Level the surface of the sand.

5. Using your hands, form a cavity in the sand to your desired shape. An oval shape looks good for this project

6. If the cavity does not retain its shape, the sand is not wet enough. Return to step 3.

The cavity is formed, and embedments placed.

7. Place the driftwood and shells around the perimeter in the desired pattern. These embedded objects should overlap partway into the mold cavity. Do not place driftwood too close to areas where wicks will be placed.

8. Once the wax is fully melted, remove it from the water pot and place it on direct heat. It is necessary to pour these candles between 300 and 325° F (149 and 163° C). Remove the wax from heat as soon as the desired pouring temperature is reached. *Warning:* These pouring temperatures require heating the wax on direct heat. A thermometer is mandatory. Never heat wax above 325° F (163° C). Do not leave it unattended at all, as the temperature will rise very fast. While the wax is on direct heat, do not be distracted by anything. If you need to answer the phone or door, remove the wax from the heat. A review of chapter 2 would be a wise idea before attempting this type of candle.

9. Put on protective clothing. Pour the wax into the mold cavity. Because of the moisture in the sand, the wax will sizzle as it enters the mold cavity. This is normal; just do not get too close in case any hot wax splatters.

10. Set aside the leftover wax for step 13.

11. When the wax on the bottom begins to solidify, insert one or more suitably sized primed and tabbed wicks. Be sure to leave a safe margin near the driftwood.

12. Allow the candle to cool until the wax is firm to the touch, yet still warm.

13. Reheat the leftover wax from step 10. The balance of the candle may be poured at 185° F (85° C), so normal double boiler heating should be used. Add color and scent if desired. A blue color looks good here.

Once the candle has cooled, dig under the edges and remove it from the sand.

14. Make the second pour. Stop pouring approximately ¼ inch (6 mm) below the level of the first pour.

15. Allow the candle to cool.

16. Remove the candle from the sand. Brush off any loose sand.

17. Optional—A torch or heat gun can be passed across the sand. This will help bond the grains of sand to the wax.

A heat gun or torch can be passed across the sand to improve adhesion.

18. If necessary, level the bottom by heating to soften the wax, then scrape the sand off until level.

19. Trim the wick(s) to ¼ inch (6 mm).

Variations

The appearance of the sand on candles can be enhanced with a variety of techniques. Here are a few suggestions:

Shape

Vary the shape of the mold cavity.

Embedding

Embed a variety of different objects.

Color

Color the first pour. This may be difficult with some colors, as the high temperature will cause some colors to shift.

Tie Dye Candles

Difficulty Rating: 9

This technique can produce some of the most beautiful candles you will ever see.

These are a lot of fun to make, and the finished product can be downright stunning. Using this technique allows us to incorporate any number of colors in the surface of the wax. We can also control the degree to which the colors blend into the fill wax, from discrete colors to a graduated color blend. The concept here is to add the colors to the mold before pouring the candle, and to place the mold into a water bath as soon as the desired amount of blending has occurred.

Materials

In addition to the materials for a plain pillar candle, you will need the following:

• Tacky wax—If you can't obtain any, beeswax may be substituted.

Formula

Colored Wax

This needs to be slightly adhesive to prevent premature separation from the mold. This can be made using 75% paraffin and 25% tacky wax. An alternative is 50% paraffin and 50% beeswax. This should be dyed to a deep color. You can prepare mulitcolors.

Fill Wax

Any pillar candle recipe may be used.

Procedure

1. Attach mold weights to the mold.

2. Place the mold in the bucket. Hold the mold down while adding water to ½ inch (13 mm) from the top of mold.

3. Remove the mold and dry any water drops that may have splashed in.

4. Melt a small amount of your colored wax formula.

5. Once the wax has melted, add color. Temperature is not critical here as long as the wax is liquid.

6. Drip a little colored wax into the mold, and immediately rotate and tilt the mold until the wax solidifies.

7. Repeat step 6 until the desired amount of that color is in the mold.

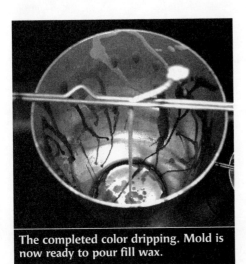

The completed color dripping. Mold is now ready to pour fill wax.

8. Repeat steps 4 through 7 for each color desired.

9. Prepare the fill wax and place it on heat.

10. Wick the mold.

11. When the wax temperature is around 190° F (88° C), pour the wax into the mold.

12. Give the mold some gentle taps with a wooden spoon to dislodge any trapped air.

13. Watch carefully until the desired amount of blending between the colored waxes and the fill wax has occurred, then continue.

14. Wearing heavy gloves, place the mold into the water bath.

15. The procedure from here is the same as for any top-down mold— poke relief holes, repour, level the base, and trim the wick.

Variations

The instructions above are for a basic tie dye candle. Other variations are possible as noted below:

Varied Color Dripping

This may be vertical, horizontal, or a mixture, depending how you tilt the mold.

Selective Color Dripping

Drip wax selectively instead of at random. For example, down the corners only.

Graduated Color Dripping

To get more color at top of candle, pour colored wax into the mold bottom. Then invert the mold and allow the wax to run down towards the mold top (which is now on the bottom). To get more color at base of candle, drip small amounts into top edge of the mold and allow the wax to run towards the bottom.

Blending

Any amount of blending from none to total is possible, depending on how quickly the mold is placed in the water bath.

Colored Fill

Although I prefer to use uncolored fill wax on these, the fill may be colored for variety.

Hurricane Shells

Difficulty Rating: 9

This is the only safe method to embed flammable objects.

Hurricane shells are some of the most beautiful candles around. In essence, they are hollow wax containers in which a smaller candle (such as a votive) is burned. When made properly, they glow from within. The shell can be filled with a nearly endless variety of embedded objects, from flowers to seashells. Because of the air space between the flame and the objects, even flammable items can be embedded with relative safety. Best of all, these works of art last for years, since the part that burns is replaceable.

Materials

The following will be needed:

- Hurricane mold—A hurricane mold is a large mold with no wick holes. Any large mold may be used by plugging the wick holes. Generally it is best not to use molds less than 5 inches (12.5 cm) in diameter.

- Hurricane mold insert—This is basically a hollow tube with no ends. They are available in a variety of sizes. The size needed is determined by the thickness of the objects you plan to embed. Use the following formula to calculate the insert size needed: *Mold size minus 2 times the embedded object thickness equals diameter of insert.* If you are on a very tight budget, a homemade insert will work almost as well. Find a suitably sized tin can and cut both ends out.

- Mold weights—These are large molds, and they may require a substantial amount of weight to keep them from floating in the water bath.

- Water bucket—A water bath is vital.

- Heavy gloves—For handling the hot mold.

- Objects to embed—See "variations" for ideas.

- Hobby knife—To cut open the surface film.

- Votive holder—To burn inside.

- Coaster—A coaster or cork sheet must be placed under the votive holder, or it will melt through the bottom when the glass heats up.

Formula

Any hurricane candle formula will work for this technique. Do not try to add Vybar or Stearic as these will make the wax opaque.

Procedure

1. Prepare the wax formula and place on a heat source.

2. Attach mold weights to the mold.

3. Place the mold in the bucket. Hold the mold down while adding water to ½ inch (13 mm) from the top of mold.

The objects to be embedded are positioned between the insert and the mold.

4. Remove the mold and dry any water drops that may have splashed in.

5. Place the insert into the mold.

6. Position the objects to be embedded between the insert and the mold.

7. When the wax temperature is around 200° F (93° C), pour the wax into the center of the insert.

The insert is removed a little at a time.

8. Allow the candle to sit for 5 minutes, giving it some gentle taps with a wooden spoon to dislodge any trapped air.

9. Wearing heavy gloves, place the mold into the water bath.

10. Immediately grasp the insert and lift it ½ inch (13 mm).

11. Wait one minute and lift the insert another ½ inch (13 mm).

The insert has been removed. Note how the embedments are held in place by the cooling wax.

12. Repeat step 11 until the insert is completely out of the mold. You will see that the hardening wax is now holding the embedded objects in place.

13. Allow to cool, while checking the wall thickness periodically. At some point you will need to cut away the surface film to see the thickness.

14. Once the wall reaches the desired thickness, remove the mold from water bath. Wall thickness is largely a matter of preference. Thin walls pass more light, but are more fragile. A thickness between ¼ and ⅜ inch (6 and 9 mm) is best.

15. Cut open and remove the surface film.

16. Pour the liquid wax out of the mold.

17. Allow the candle to cool.

18. Level the top edge the same way you would normally level the bottom of a candle. If any embedded objects floated to the top, it may be necessary to trim them with a razor before leveling.

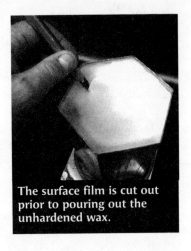

The surface film is cut out prior to pouring out the unhardened wax.

19. To use, place a coaster or piece of cork under the votive holder and place them inside the hurricane shell.

Variations

The basic hurricane shell may be enhanced in a variety of ways; here are a few suggestions to get you started:

Colored Drips

Make a translucent shell, and then drip colored wax on the inside.

Chunks

Embed colored wax chunks.

Potpourri

Embed potpourri.

Flowers

Embed dried or silk flowers.

Candy

Embed hard candy, or candy canes.

Seashells

Embed thin seashells. Warning—this may scratch the mold.

Beans

Embed coffee beans or other types of dried beans.

Cinnamon

Embed cinnamon sticks or chips.

Paper

Embed decorative paper. This does not require an insert. The paper is cut to fit and held in place with spring clothespins.

Candle

To make a large candle, place a wick inside and slowly fill with wax as explained for balloon candles. Not recommended when using flammable embedded objects.

Hurricane Candles—Method 1

Difficulty Rating: 9

Hurricane candles are similar to hurricane shells in that they may contain embedded objects and glow from within. In essence, they are large candles with objects embedded in them. Because there is no air space between the flame and the objects, I strongly suggest that flammable items not be embedded. This is especially true for small (3 inch or less diameter) candles. I have seen quite a few of these burst into raging infernos when the embedded objects caught fire (they can act as giant wicks). Even on large candles, flammable objects are not totally safe.

Materials

Candy canes were used here because they have a relatively low flammability, although they will burn.

In addition to the materials for a standard pillar candle, the following will be needed:

Large mold—A mold 4 inches (10 cm) in diameter or larger is best. The larger the better.

Smaller mold—This mold should be the same height as the large mold and smaller in diameter. The size needed is determined by the thickness of the objects you plan to embed. Use the following formula to calculate the insert size needed: *Mold size minus 2 times the embedded object thickness equals diameter needed.* For a 5 inch mold with ½ inch thick embedded objects, we would need a 4 inch diameter mold.

Objects to embed—Use non-flammable objects.

Formula

For the smaller candle use any standard pillar candle formula. For the outer layer use any hurricane candle formula. Do not use Vybar or stearic in the outer layer, as these will make the wax opaque.

Procedure

1. Make a basic pillar candle in the smaller mold. This must be complete before proceeding, so it helps to plan ahead. Level the base, but do not trim the wick, as a longer wick will simplify step 3.

This photo was taken just after pouring. Note how the smaller candle in the center holds the embedments in placed.

2. Start heating your hurricane wax formula.

3. Thread the wick of the candle from step 1 through the wick hole of the larger mold from the inside. This will position the smaller candle in the center of the large mold.

4. Seal the wick hole with putty-type mold sealer.

5. Position objects to be embedded between the candle and the mold.

6. When the wax temperature is around 200° F (93° C), pour the wax into the perimeter of the mold. Make sure the candle and embedded objects are covered.

7. Give the mold some gentle taps with a wooden spoon to dislodge any trapped air.

8. Allow the candle to cool. Due to the small volume of heated wax at this stage, a water bath is unnecessary.

9. Once the candle is fully cooled, remove it from the mold.

10. Level the base.

11. Trim the wick to ¼ inch (6 mm).

Variants

The basic hurricane candle may be enhanced in a variety of ways; here are a few suggestions to get you started:

Objects

Embed a variety of non-flammable objects.

Colored Drips

Drip colored wax on the inside candle before placing, then fill the mold with translucent wax with no embedded objects. This works best when the inner candle is only slightly smaller, as it puts the color closer to the surface. Reduce pouring temperature to 185° (85° C) to prevent melting the colored wax off with this technique. A water bath may also be needed to cool the wax before it melts the colored wax.

Colored Shell

Lightly color the hurricane wax.

Colored Candle

Color the inner candle.

Chunks

Embed colored wax chunks.

Candy

Embed hard candy or candy canes. Although they can burn, they are not porous enough to become wicks and are moderately safe.

Hurricane Candles—Method 2

Difficulty Rating:10

This is another technique for making hurricane candles. Rather than repeat what you have just read, I will just discuss the points where this technique differs. Everything said about hurricane candles applies here as well.

Materials

In addition to the materials for a standard pillar candle the following will be needed:

- Large mold—A mold 4 inches (10 cm) in diameter or larger is best. The larger the better.

- Hurricane mold insert—This is basically a hollow tube with no ends. They are available in a variety of sizes. The size needed is determined by the thickness of the objects you plan to embed. Use the following formula to calculate the insert size needed: *Mold size minus 2 times the embedded object thickness equals diameter of insert.* If you are on a very tight budget, a homemade insert will work almost as well. Find a suitably sized tin can and cut both ends out.

This candle was made with cinnamon sticks, which are flammable—I consider this for decoration only and would not burn or sell a candle like this due to the fire hazard.

- Mold weights—These are large molds and they may require a substantial amount of weight to keep them from floating in the water bath.

- Water bucket—A water bath is vital.

- Heavy gloves—For handling the hot mold.

- Objects to embed—Use non-flammable objects.

Formula

For these hurricane candles use any standard pillar candle formula. Use a wick appropriate to a substantially smaller diameter mold (we don't want it to burn all the way to the embedded objects).

Procedure

1. Start heating your wax formula.

2. Attach mold weights to the mold.

3. Place the mold in the bucket. Hold the mold down while adding water to ½ inch (13 mm) from the top of mold.

4. Remove the mold and dry any water drops that may have splashed in.

5. Insert the wick through the hurricane insert. Leave a long length of wick—approximately 2½ times the length of the insert. To minimize waste, I usually just leave the entire spool so that the unused wick may be wound back up.

6. Thread the end of the wick through the wick hole from the inside.

7. Seal the wick hole.

8. Place the insert in the mold. Do not fasten the wick to the wick bar at this point.

9. Position the objects to be embedded between the candle and the mold.

10. When the wax temperature is around 200° F (93° C), pour the wax into the center of the insert.

The cinnamon sticks are placed around the insert.

11. Give the mold some gentle taps with a wooden spoon to dislodge any trapped air. Allow the mold to sit for about 5 minutes.

12. Wearing heavy gloves, place the mold into the water bath.

13. Immediately grasp the insert and lift it ½ inch (13 mm).

14. Wait one minute and lift the insert another ½ inch (13 mm).

The insert removed and wick positioned.

15. Repeat step 14 until the insert is completely out of the mold. You will see that the hardening wax is now holding the embedded objects in place.

16. It is now time to cut the wick and attach it to a wick bar. Make sure it is centered.

17. The procedure from here is the same as for any top-down mold—pour the wax to fill the mold, poke relief holes, repour, level the base, and trim the wick.

Experimenting

I have tried to present all the basic techniques of candle embellishment in these project chapters. At this point you should have a firm grasp of all the basic (and not so basic) techniques used to add variety to plain candles. I need to point out that it doesn't end there, because many of these techniques may be combined to create further variants. Let your creativity go.

19

Experimenting

𝓘 cannot stress enough the importance of experimentation and
record-keeping for the development of a well-made candle. Most of
the candles seen in stores today are the result of extensive experimentation. There are no magic formulas, no arcane rituals, and no candle fairy
that can wave her wand and make your candles come out well. There is an
unlimited number of ways in which candle materials may be combined,
and many will produce a good candle with a bit of experimentation.

Do not be put off by this—experimenting is fun. Playing with different
materials, trying new techniques, and developing new styles are enjoyable
ways to pass some time. Experimentation can be rewarding as well.
Improving burn time, scent throw, appearance, and just increasing your
candle making knowledge in general are some of the benefits of experimenting. The key to experimenting is test burning the candles. As you read
through this chapter, it may seem like a lot of test burning is needed. But
then again, if you didn't enjoy burning candles, you probably wouldn't be

reading this book.

Develop a basic formula for each type of candle—pillar, container, votive, floater—that you wish to make. A basic formula/wick combination that works well for a standard size is vital as a jumping off point for further experimentation. Consider this the yardstick by which you will measure the quality of experiment results.

When experimenting, change only one thing per experiment. For example, if you try a new wax and a new scent in the same candle, you will not know which caused any problems, or improvements.

Record Keeping

There is little point in experimenting if you don't keep a record of what you do. Nothing is more frustrating than coming up with a perfect candle and not being able to reproduce the results. Keep a record of all ingredients, temperatures, mold, wicks, any special steps or techniques, and who the supplier was for each material. I have included a sample record sheet in Appendix B. When you achieve the desired results, the record sheet may be added to a recipe book for ease of reference.

Experimental Procedure—Wax Formula

In your initial candle making endeavors, I recommend using the formulas in this book. I have been using them for many years and I know they work well. Since the properties of some materials, such as wax and scent oil, vary from one supplier to the next, recipes from any source may need to be modified unless you are using the same suppliers. If you need to use different materials, that is okay, but be prepared to experiment.

To test your materials with an existing formula (recipe):

1. Make a candle with the formula. Do a test burn. If the results are acceptable, use the formula as is; otherwise, go to step 2.

2. Try a few different wick sizes. This will usually solve the problem. If the results are acceptable, use the formula as is; otherwise, go to step 3.

3. Analyze the results you are obtaining. Does the wax need to be harder or softer? Change the amount of hardener accordingly, and do another test burn.

4. Repeat step 3 until the desired results are obtained.

To develop a formula from scratch (or just to play around with different additives), first choose a wax with a melt point appropriate to the type of candle you wish to make. Then choose an additive that will aid in what you wish to accomplish. The more thought you put into additive choice, the better your results will be. For example, to make a pillar formula you would choose a hardening additive. For a sculpting wax you might choose an additive that increases flexibility. Start with only one additive.

If the formula is to be used for scented candles, the scent oil must be added even to experimental candles. This may seem like a waste of expensive scent oil, but keep in mind that the scent oil affects the burning by changing the viscosity (thickness) of the melted wax. The thicker the liquid wax, the larger the wick required. Most quality dyes, on the other hand, will have little or no effect on the burning properties unless very large amounts of dye are used; you can usually safely leave the dye out of test candles.

Make a candle with your test formula. Allow it to cure for a minimum of 24 hours, then test burn it. If the results are good, you have a new formula. If results are fair, try a few different wick sizes as explained below. If results are poor, try again with either a different amount of additive or a different additive.

Experimental Procedure—Fun Time

When experimenting for the fun of it, just let your imagination go. Wax is a very versatile substance. If you can envision something, there is usually a way to make a candle that looks like your vision. This type of experimentation is generally more useful for creating new candle styles.

Experimental Procedure—Burn Time/Scent Throw

Once you have a wax formula that you like, it is necessary to play with wicks to obtain optimum burn and scent throw. This should only need to be done once for each size mold. This only applies to molds of different diameters or shapes: the height of a straight-sided mold only affects the length of the wick. Test burning candles that are identical except for wick size can be very illuminating (pardon the pun). For years I made small floaters with 28-24 sp. wicks, figuring the smallest size would burn longest. One day I had just poured a batch when I realized I was out of my usual wick. I had some 34-40 wicks handy and surprise! They burned almost an hour longer. Even though the wicks were larger, they used more of the wax by melting a larger diameter and so burned longer. Since that time I have always tested new mold sizes with at least three different size wicks—the one I think will be best, one size smaller, and one size larger.

This process is fairly straightforward; make candles that are identical except for the wick size. Allow them to sit for a minimum of twenty-four hours before testing. Make sure you keep track of which wick is in which candle. Test burn them for at least 1 hour per inch in diameter. For example, a 3-inch (7.5 cm) candle should be burned a minimum of 3 hours at a time. I prefer to burn all the test candles at once so I can compare their melt pools as well as burn times. The melt pool is one of the most important factors for a good scent throw—the more liquid wax, the more scent is released.

Factors to Bear in Mind

There are few standards in the candle industry in regards to the composition of the supplies we use. The following explains some of the differences.

Waxes

All paraffin waxes are not created equal. This is not to imply that some are good and some are bad, just that they are different. Personal preference is more of a factor in what is good and bad. What I consider a great wax, others may think is terrible and vice versa. Most waxes have different properties; sometimes minimal, sometimes big. For example, if you took wax with a melt point of 130° F from ten different suppliers, you would find that most have different properties. Some will not work well with your existing formulas, while others will. For best results, find a wax you like and stick with it.

Additives

Not too many years ago there was basically one additive available to us— stearic acid. As the popularity of candles has boomed, so has the number of additives currently available to the candle maker. Many of us now get caught up in developing complex wax formulas. Avoid this—use an additive only if there is a logical reason for it. I see many candle makers using both stearic and Vybar, for example—when I ask why, they cannot offer a logical explanation. I have a thriving candle business, and rarely do I use more than one additive. Keeping your formulas simple makes them easier to mix, troubleshoot, change, and experiment with.

Scent

As with paraffin waxes, there are no standards. The "same" scent oil will smell different and have different properties from one supplier to the next. Even different scent oils from the same supplier may have different properties, but these differences are usually less pronounced than those between different suppliers. In practical terms, this means that testing and reformulating either the wax, the scent percentage, or the wick might be needed whenever changing scent oils. This is especially true when using scent oils from different suppliers.

Color

Most of the commercial candle dyes currently available work quite well and should have little bearing on how your candle burns. If you experience wick clogging, it can usually be attributed to using a pigment dye. Switching to an oil-soluble candle dye should correct the problem.

Wick

Use a good quality wick. String, rope, shoelaces, and such will usually give results that are inferior to braided cotton wicking. Guidelines on wick packaging are just that—guidelines. Your wax formula may need a larger or smaller wick. Experimentation is the only way to determine the exact wick size needed. It is usually best to settle on a wax formula, and then adjust wick size to fine tune the burning properties. Wick selection is the most important part of a candle, so an entire chapter of this book has been devoted to wicking (chapter 8).

20

Wax Recycling

While you are candle making keep in mind that wax is highly recyclable and is not unusable until it has finally been consumed by flames. Most folks with an interest in candle making have at one time or another remelted old candles and drippings to make new candles (with varying results). With the proper recycling strategy, you will be able to make more effective use of scrap wax and save yourself some money.

What should you save? Everything! Failed experiments, drippings, partially used candles, etc. You can find a use for it all.

Recycling Strategy

The following are general guidelines for recycling wax. Obviously, not all of the points mentioned will be practical for everyone. The more candles you make, the more of the following will apply.

Substantial quantities of wax should be poured into a pan. I use 8-inch (20 cm) square cake pans for this. Once cooled, scribe the type of formula and fragrance into the wax surface with a knifepoint or ice pick. Simply incorporate this wax the next time you need that fragrance in that formula. This may also be done with candles used for test burning. By using the same size pan for all of these, storage is simplified. I always use the same color for each fragrance when mixing my formulas to simplify reuse and minimize waste.

Small quantities of wax should be poured into a small container or mold. I use a floater mold for floating candle formulas, votive mold for votive formulas, a small pie pan for pillar formulas, etc. By doing this I can tell at a glance what the formula of my scrap wax is, so all I need to do is scribe the fragrance into the wax surface.

Tiny amounts of wax can be placed in a container or bag. Any wax that is of unknown formula (such as remnants of candles that you didn't make) should be kept with this group as well. If you have the space, separate these by color family, i.e., reds, yellows, blues, and so on. When colors are mixed, the result is usually in the brown family, so this will give you more flexibility when you use the wax.

Reusing Wax

The following suggestions will help you use up all the wax you save in the most economical manner.

- Whenever you mix up a batch of wax, check your recycle bin for any in the same formula/fragrance to incorporate into your current batch of wax.

- When I have accumulated enough small pieces of scrap, I make a chunk candle with them. Please remember that the chunks will all need to be the same formula, the fill wax will have to be the same formula as the chunks, and the wick size may need to be modified accordingly.

- Ugly votives; if you make a lot of votives, this is an ideal way to use up scraps without having to store them. Set up six or more votive molds in your work area. Any wax remaining after pouring votives is then poured into these molds, giving each a thin layer. This is repeated as you have leftovers from other batches until the mold is full. A wick needs to be inserted on the first pour. These layered, multi-scented votives are fairly popular. They lack the perfection of form that a normal votive has, appearing as a layered cold-poured candle.

• Combine small scraps of different scents to make complete candles. This works best when you know the formula of the wax. If the wax is of an unknown pedigree you may still try this method; however, some trial and error will be needed to determine the best wick size.

• Citronella candles are a great use for scrap wax. Since they are used outdoors to repel insects, they don't have to burn perfectly. As a matter of fact, the more they smoke the better they work, so use an oversize wick. By using scented wax scraps, they also have a less offensive smell.

• Make fire starters. The wax formula is irrelevant for these, so you can use up any wax that is otherwise unsuitable for candle making. At my shop, we scrape hundreds of pounds of dripped wax off the floor every year. I would never use this filthy wax in a candle, but after straining the dirt I use it to make fire starters.

Fire starters are a great way to light campfires, wood burning stoves, and fireplaces. They can be made by pouring scrap wax into cardboard egg cartons to obtain a 100 percent recycled product. To use, simply separate one section and light the torn edge with a match. They will produce a large flame for about 15 minutes—long enough to ignite damp wood.

Cleaning Wax

Recycled wax tends to have a variety of contaminants such as dirt, carbon, wick pieces, etc., if it comes from drippings and used candles. This is not as much of a problem on wax left over from pouring candles. The following process is the simplest way I have found to remove contaminants.

1. If remelting candles, cut off the charred portion of the wick.

2. Melt the wax.

3. Place a paper towel in a strainer.

4. Place the strainer atop another pot.

5. Pour the melted wax through the strainer.

If you prefer, the paper towel may be placed directly on the second pot. Push it into the pot as far as possible, while leaving enough paper towel overlapping the rim to hold it in place with a rubber band.

21

Wax Formulas

Throughout this book I have mentioned a variety of different wax formulas or recipes. I have also discussed at some length how materials from different suppliers will most likely have different properties. I understand that this may be confusing to those just getting started in candle making. All of the formulas included here I have used successfully, and they were chosen for ease of preparation and availability of materials. Since many of you reading this book may not be using the same exact materials as I use, some slight adjustments to the formulas presented may occasionally be necessary.

Those readers outside the United States may find difficulty obtaining some of the materials mentioned. I have provided some formulas using only the most basic of candle making supplies to help overcome supply difficulties. Although these may not be the most advanced wax formulas around, they will work.

As you read through this chapter, you will note that there is not much difference between my formulas for various types of candles. Here are the reasons:

• I firmly believe every word in this book, so in keeping with my philosophy of keeping things simple, I do. Complicated formulas don't impress me, but good results do.

• If a formula works well for one type of candle, a modified version of it will probably work well for most candle types.

• If I used a different wax and additive for each type of candle I make, I would have a lot more items to order, stock, keep track of inventory, etc. As long as I can make a top quality candle with the materials on hand, why should I increase the effort of maintaining a ready supply of the materials I need?

The formulas given below are in order of my preference from my favorite to least favorite in each category. Please note that the volume measures are approximate. Weights are given also, and are much more accurate to use if you have a decent scale. The scent oil amounts given are typical, and may need to be adjusted up or down depending on your scent oil and the level of scenting desired. Scent oil may be omitted for unscented candles.

Container Candles

Container candles can be the simplest candles to make. On the other hand, many beginners find them frustrating to make. A lot depends on how you approach them. A properly made container candle will liquefy very quickly, providing a deep melt pool to release lots of fragrance. Additionally, it will burn all the way across (not leaving any substantial amount of unmelted wax on the sides). Finally, it will burn with a minimal amount of mushrooming (carbon buildup) on the wick.

I have included some formulas here, but I personally use a preblended container wax. The main advantage of blended container waxes is much less shrinkage than other formulas. They generally have a low melt point for improved scent throw (larger melt pool), and are convenient because all you need to add is scent and color. Their manufacturers generally consider the formulas of blended waxes trade secrets, so I cannot enlighten you on their ingredients. I can tell you that some blended waxes work quite well, while others are absolutely terrible. I suggest trying small quantities and drawing your own conclusions.

Container Formula One

1 pound (454 grams) pre blended container wax
2 tablespoons (28.3 ml) scent oil (1 ounce or 28.3 grams)
Dye—to desired color

Container Formula Two

1 pound (454 grams) 130° F (60° C) paraffin wax
1 level teaspoon (4.7 ml) Vybar 260 (3.2 grams)
2 tablespoons (28.3 ml) scent oil (1 ounce or 28.3 grams)
Dye—to desired color

Container Formula Three

1 pound (454 grams) 130° F (60° C) paraffin wax
3 tablespoons (42 ml) stearic acid (1 ounce or 28.3 grams). The
 amount needed for good results will vary with different waxes.
2 tablespoons (28.3 ml) scent oil (1 ounce or 28.3 grams if using a scale).
 This amount may need to be reduced to prevent mottling.
Dye—to desired color

Floating Candles

For floating candles we need a hard formula. This will help the burn time, because the sides will have enough strength to resist the water pressure even once thinned by burning. Although they can be scented, the scent throw will never be as good as that obtained from a votive or container candle since it will have a substantially smaller melt pool.

Floating Candle Formula One

1 pound (454 grams) 140° F (60°C) paraffin wax
2 level teaspoons (9.4 ml) Vybar 103 (6.4 grams)
2 tablespoons (28.3 ml) scent oil (1 ounce or 28.3 grams)
Dye—to desired color

Floating Candle Formula Two

1 pound (454 grams) 140° degree F (60° C) paraffin wax
6 to 9 tablespoons (84 to 127 ml) stearic acid (2 to 3 ounces or 56.6 to 127.4 grams). This amount needed for good results will vary with different waxes.
2 tablespoons (28.3 ml) scent oil (1 ounce or 28.3 grams). Note: this amount may need to be reduced to prevent mottling.
Dye—to desired color.

Floating Candle Formula Three

1 pound (454 grams) 140° F (60° C) paraffin wax.
1½ level teaspoons (7 ml) luster crystals (7 grams)
2 tablespoons (28.3 ml) scent oil (1 ounce or 28.3 grams)
Dye—to desired color.

Hurricane Candles

For hurricane candles we need a very hard formula to prevent heat damage from the core candle. This is somewhat complicated by the need for translucency in most hurricanes. Although there is quite a variety of hardeners that will make the wax opaque, there are not many that will leave the wax translucent.

Hurricane Formula One

1 pound (454 grams) 140°F (60° C) paraffin wax
0.8 to 3.2 ounces (20 to 81 grams) Micro 180 (this is marketed under a variety of names, but ask your supplier for a high temperature microcrystalline wax)
Scent—not recommended.
Dye—to desired color

Hurricane Formula Two

1 pound (454 grams) 140° F (60° C) paraffin wax
1 level teaspoon (4.7 ml) clear crystals (0.1 ounce or 3.2 grams). This
will need to be melted separately and stirred into the wax due to its
high melt point.
Scent—not recommended
Dye—to desired color

Over-Dipping Candles

For over-dipping we basically just need a wax that will provide a smooth dipped coat with no adhesion problems. I normally use formula one, but for white candles I use formula two as it is more opaque.

Over-Dip Formula One

1 pound (454 grams) 140° F (60° C) paraffin wax
Scent oil—not recommended
Pigment—to desired color. Due to the thinness of the dipped coating,
dyes will usually not provide sufficient depth of color, so pigments
are used instead.

Over-Dip Formula Two

1 pound (454 grams) 140° F (60° C) paraffin wax
3 tablespoons (42 ml) stearic acid (1 ounce or 28.3 grams)
Scent oil—not recommended
Pigment—to desired color

Pillar/Molded Candles

For pillar candles we need a relatively hard formula to prevent the candle from sagging in warm weather. If we are to have decent scent throw, a good melt pool is desirable. These two requirements are somewhat contradictory, so we have to settle on a formula that is somewhat of a compromise. The scent throw will never be as good as that obtained from a votive or container candle, since it will have a substantially smaller melt pool.

Pillar Formula One

1 pound (454 grams) 140° F (60° C) paraffin wax
1 level teaspoon (4.7 ml) Vybar 103 (3.2 grams)
2 tablespoons (28.3 ml) scent oil (1 ounce or 28.3 grams)
Dye—to desired color

Pillar Formula Two

1 pound (454 grams) 140° F (60° C) paraffin wax.
3 to 9 tablespoons (42 to 127 ml) stearic acid (1 to 3 ounces or 28.3 to 127.4 grams.) The amount needed for good results will vary with different waxes. In no instance should less than 3 tablespoons be used.
2 tablespoons (28.3 ml) scent oil (1 ounce or 28.3 grams). This amount may need to be reduced to prevent mottling.
Dye—to desired color

Pillar Formula Three

1 pound (454 grams) 140° F (60° C) paraffin wax
½ to1 level teaspoon (2.3 to 4.7 ml) luster crystals (1.6 to 3.2 grams)
2 tablespoons (28.3 ml) scent oil (1 ounce or 28.3 grams)
Dye—to desired color

Sculpting Wax

On occasion you may need a wax that is more flexible than is usually possible with paraffin. Sculpting formulas also tend to be a bit more adhesive than standard wax formulas. A good sculpting formula will be quite flexible and easily worked when warm, but fairly hard when fully cooled.

Sculpting Formula One

½ pound (227 grams) 140° degree F (60° C) paraffin wax
½ pound (227 grams) of bleached beeswax (bleached beeswax is white and does not affect color as much as natural beeswax)
Scent—Do not scent, the oils reduce adhesive properties.
Dye—to desired color. Pigments may be used if it is not a core candle.

Sculpting Formula Two

1 pound (454 grams) of 140° F (60° C) paraffin wax
1.6 to 8 ounces (45 to 227 grams) of tacky wax. This is from 10 to 50 percent. Use the least amount possible to obtain the desired amount of flexibility/adhesiveness.
Scent—Do not scent; the oils reduce adhesive properties.
Dye—to desired color. Pigments may also be used if it will not be used for a core candle.

Taper Candles

For dipped tapers we need a relatively hard formula to prevent the candle from sagging in warm weather. Normally tapers are not scented, so scent throw is not a consideration. I only have one formula for dipped tapers since I do not like the results with any high-tech additives.

Taper Formula

1 pound (454 grams) 140° F (60° C) paraffin wax
3 tablespoons (42 ml) stearic acid (1 ounce or 28.3 grams). For use where sagging may be a problem, you may wish to increase the amount of stearic. In no instance should less than 3 tablespoons be used.
Scent Oil—not recommended
Dye—to desired color

Votive Candles

Votives are an oddball in the candle world. Although commonly mistaken for small pillar candles, they are essentially container candles and will only burn properly in a container. A properly made votive will liquefy very quickly, providing a deep melt pool to release lots of fragrance. I have included four formulas here. The first two release fragrance the best, but are susceptible to warm temperatures and are prone to melt together in storage if the temperature approaches 100° F (38° C). The second two do not release fragrance quite as well, but are more durable in hot climates.

Cool Climate Votive Formula One

1 pound (454 grams) 130°F (60° C) paraffin wax
1 level teaspoon (4.7 ml) Vybar 260 (3.2 grams if using a scale)
2 tablespoons (28.3ml.) Scent Oil (1 ounce or 28.3 grams if using a scale)
Dye—to desired color.

Cool Climate Votive Formula Two

1 pound (454 grams) 130° F (60° C) paraffin wax
3 tablespoons (42 ml) stearic acid (1 ounce or 28.3 grams). The amount needed for good results will vary with different waxes.
2 tablespoons (28.3 ml) scent oil (1 ounce or 28.3 grams). This amount may need to be reduced to prevent mottling.
Dye—to desired color

Warm Climate Votive Formula One

1 pound (454 grams) 140° F (60° C) paraffin wax
1 level teaspoon (4.7 ml) Vybar 103 (3.2 grams)
2 tablespoons (28.3 ml) scent oil (1 ounce or 28.3 grams)
Dye—to desired color.

Warm Climate Votive Formula Two

1 pound (454 grams) 140° F (60° C) paraffin wax.
3 tablespoons (42 ml) stearic acid (1 ounce or 28.3 grams). The amount needed for good results will vary with different waxes.
2 tablespoons (28.3 ml) scent oil (1 ounce or 28.3 grams). This amount may need to be reduced to prevent mottling

Glossary

In the course of discussing candle making many terms and abbreviations are used. It is important to know the meanings of the following terms to prevent confusion when reading or discussing various topics. I have put this glossary together to help all candle makers to have a common language.

Additives—Anything added to the wax. Examples include stearic, Vybar, polythenes, etc. Although technically additives, colorants and scents are not normally included in this category when discussing candles.

Appliqué—This is the process of applying an item to the surface of the finished candle. It can also be used to describe the actual item to be applied. Appliquéd items of any material such as wax, paper, flowers, fabric, etc.

Beeswax—A natural wax derived from honeybee hives.

Beeswax Sheets—Beeswax that has been formed into ready-to-use sheets. Available in colors and natural. Although usually found with a honeycomb pattern, some suppliers offer smooth sheets as well.

Burn time—How long a candle burns until exhausted.

Celsius—The standard temperature measuring system for most of the world. Abbreviated as C when following a temperature.

Chatter marks—*See stuttering.*

Chunk—A small piece of colored wax used to create chunk candles. May be uniform or irregular.

Container—Used to describe anything a candle is poured in that is to be used as part of the finished candle (as opposed to a mold, from which the candle is removed before use).

Cookie cutter—Metal or plastic shapes made for cutting cookie dough. May be used to cut sheet wax.

Core—The central part of a candle. Most simple candles have just a core. More elaborate or dipped candles may have an outer layer over the core.

Dipping—The process of dipping a candle into either wax or water.

Double boiler—This is the only safe way to melt wax without special equipment. This may be a commercially made double boiler or simply a smaller pot (holding wax) placed inside a larger pot that contains water.

Dye—Wax colorants that are oil soluble, used for core coloring. Please note: contrary to popular opinion, most children's crayons do not make good candle dyes.

EO—A common abbreviation for essential oil.

Essential oil—Natural oils extracted from plant matter. Most essential oils are difficult to use in candles.

Farenheit—The standard temperature measuring system in the United States. Abbreviated as F when following a temperature.

FO—A common abbreviation for fragrance oil.

Formula—*See wax formula.*

Fragrance Oil—A synthetic oil or combination of synthetic and natural oils. Often referred to as scent oil. There are many different types, and those designed specifically for candles work best. Typical usage is one ounce per pound for a heavily scented candle, although some oils may require more or less.

Granulated—A term usually used when referring to wax. Granulated wax has been run through a granulator instead of a slabbing machine. Granulating does not change the properties of the liquid wax that is run through the granulator, although it is generally easier to use.

Hurricane—A true hurricane candle is a wax shell in which a smaller candle is burned. The name derives from hurricane lanterns, which are kerosene lanterns that have a glass tube over the wick (making them wind resistant, hence the term hurricane lamps). In recent years the term has also come to include filled hurricane shells (hurricane candles). Although somewhat of a misnomer, it is common practice to call both styles hurricane candles.

Layering—This is the process of pouring multiple layers of colored wax.

Leveling—The process of melting off high spots to create a flat surface on the candle. Usually applied to the bottom of the candle, but in some instances may be applied to the top.

Melt point—The melting point of the wax. This is the primary way to differentiate between different waxes, i.e., *low, medium,* and *high melting point.* Remember that waxes with the same melt point do not necessarily have the same properties, and actual properties will vary from supplier to supplier. Melt point is commonly confused with pouring temperature, but has little or no relation to the pouring temperature required.

Melt pool—The liquid puddle of wax that forms around the wick when burning a candle.

Mold—Anything used to form a candle that is not an integral part of the candle (it is removed before burning).

Mold plugs—Rubber plugs used to seal wick holes in molds.

Mold sealer—A putty-like substance used to seal wick holes in molds.

Mold weight—A piece of metal that is wrapped around the bottom of molds to prevent the mold from floating or tipping when placed in a water bath. Commercial mold weights are made of lead, and you should wash your hands after handling them.

Mottling—A blotched appearance in the wax. Often has the look of snowflakes. Although this was once considered a defect, it has become a popular style of candle.

MP—Common abbreviation for melt point or melting point.

Over-dip—Dipping a core candle in wax to add color or other effects. Sometimes done with hot water.

Paraffin—The most common candle making wax. Refined from petroleum.

Pigment—Non–oil soluble wax colorants. These consist of colored particles that are suspended in the wax. Used only for over-dipping. Use in the core candle may clog the wick.

Pillar Candle—A free standing candle in a geometric shape. I have also seen these referred to as block candles. Although many people think of pillar candles as round, they may also be square, hexagonal, star-shaped, oval, etc. Additionally, they may be straight-sided or tapered.

Pouring temperature—The temperature the candle is poured at. Commonly abbreviated as pour temp or pouring temp. The type of mold will usually determine this, although sometimes special effects require specific pouring temperatures. Pouring temperature is commonly confused with melt point, but has little or no relation to melt point.

Priming—The coating of wicking with wax.

Recipe—The instructions needed for that type of candle. A recipe will usually include a wax formula. The projects in this book may be considered recipes.

Scent oil—A term used interchangeably with fragrance oil.

Slab—A block of wax. Usually between 10 and 12 pounds. Most suppliers offer wax in slab form.

Stuttering—Also called chattering. Usually caused by pouring too cool, or pouring into a mold that is too cold. The wax alternately flows and cools going up the sides of the mold or container causing horizontal lines and air bubbles in the finished candle.

Water bath—The placing of filled molds in water to improve surface finish and to speed cooling.

Wax crystals—Granulated wax that has color, hardeners, and other additives already added. Do not confuse these with pure granulated paraffin. Sometimes called wax art crystals.

Wax formula—The entire wax mixture. The formula includes the wax(es), additives, dyes, and fragrances. Both the ingredients and amounts should be recorded for future use. Formulas are for a specific type of candle such as pillar, container, votive, etc.

Whipped wax—Wax that has been whipped with a whisk or blender to introduce air into the mixture.

Appendix

Candle Making Record Sheet

The following is a sample of the information you should keep track of when experimenting. Obviously you will not fill every line for each candle. The final version of this sheet can be added to your recipe book, and will contain much useful information such as how much wax is needed for that mold, the formula, how long it will take to make, where to reorder materials when needed, and so on.

Candle Making Record Sheet

Additive_____   Quantity_____   Supplier_____

Additive_____   Quantity_____   Supplier_____

Additive_____   Quantity_____   Supplier_____

Scent_____   Quantity_____   Supplier_____

Color_____   Quantity_____   Supplier_____

Additive_____   Quantity_____   Supplier_____

Scent_____   Quantity_____   Supplier_____

Color_____   Quantity_____   Supplier_____

Wick_____   Supplier_____

Pouring Temperature   _____

Time to Second Pour   _____

Total Cooling Time   _____

Mold Fill Weight (weigh finished candle)   _____

Special Techniques and Notes_____

_____

_____

_____